CLAIRE RICHARDS

ALL OF ME

Visit www.panmacmillan.com to read more about all of our books
and to buy them. You will also find features, author interviews and
news of any author events, and you can sign up for e-newsletters
so that you're always first to hear about our new releases.

PAN BOOKS

First published 2012 by Sidgwick & Jackson

First published in paperback 2013 by Pan Books
an imprint of Pan Macmillan, a division of Macmillan Publishers Limited
Pan Macmillan, 20 New Wharf Road, London N1 9RR
Basingstoke and Oxford
Associated companies throughout the world
www.panmacmillan.com

ISBN 978-1-4472-1741-1

A CIP catalogue record for this book is available from
the British Library.

Typeset by Ellipsis Digital Limited, Glasgow
Printed and bound by CPI Group (UK) Ltd, Croydon, CR0 4YY

CONTENTS

For Reece, Charlie and Daisy – you make my life complete.
I love you. xx

Picture Acknowledgements

Section one – Page 4, bottom: Ilpo Musto/Rex Features;
page 7, top: Richard Young/Rex Features;
page 7, bottom: P. Rosenbaum/scopefeatures.com;
page 8, top right: Getty Images.

Section two – Page 1, top left: Brian Rasic/Rex Features;
page 2, top: Shine TV Ltd; page 3, top and bottom: WOMAN/Paul Mitchell;
page 5, bottom right: James Curley/Rex Features;
page 6: ITV/Rex Features;
page 8, top and bottom: Ken McKay/Rex Features.

Every effort has been made to contact the copyright holders of
photographs reproduced in this book. If any have been inadvertently
overlooked, the publisher will be happy to make restitution
at the earliest opportunity.

PROLOGUE

SECOND CHANCES

Standing backstage at the Belfast Odyssey Arena, I can hear the roar of the crowd and I feel that familiar tingle of excitement running through my veins. It's such an emotional moment for me and I'm trying desperately hard to hold back the tears and keep my composure. I don't want to ruin my make-up!

I never thought I'd be back here again, standing next to my bandmates Ian 'H' Watkins, Lee Latchford Evans, Faye Tozer and Lisa Scott-Lee, waiting to perform to a packed arena on the first night of our 2012 reunion tour.

I'm feeling ridiculously happy and really nervous, too, but I know when I get out there and the music starts, my nerves will disappear and it'll be amazing. Singing is my passion and I've missed it like hell.

It feels a world away from the last time I was in this position. On the last night of our 'Gold: Greatest Hits' tour in

December 2001, I was in bits as I walked out on stage at Manchester's MEN Arena. I'd just resigned from the band and I couldn't stop the tears from falling because I knew it was going to be the last time I'd perform with Steps. I also knew it would mean the end of the band.

Most people thought I was crazy for walking away. We were at the height of our success and had a number-one album at the time. But I just couldn't do it any more. The atmosphere in the band was toxic – we were barely talking to each other – and I was more miserable than I'd ever been in my life. It was no longer about the singing as, sadly, that had been overtaken by band politics and petty rivalries.

I was just nineteen when I won a place in Steps and, looking back, I was ill-equipped to deal with the pressure that comes with being in such a successful pop group and I didn't have the self-confidence to speak up for myself. To top it all, I'd been literally starving myself for years to be the perfect skinny blonde pop star the industry wanted me to be.

It was exhausting, and I believed the only way to be truly happy was to walk away from it all and start again. I had to get out to save myself.

'Claire, let me just adjust this strap for you,' says our stylist, fiddling with my costume. 'There you go. Perfect! You look gorgeous.'

'Yeah, not bad!' I think, checking myself in the full-length mirror.

*

Ten years ago I would have been wearing my trademark outfit of skimpy bra top and hipsters, but my first stage outfit tonight is a sexy black catsuit, which is low cut and nipped in at the waist, hugging my curves. I feel good.

It's taken years for me to feel happier with my shape. When the band broke up I overindulged in my other passion in life – food. I sat on my sofa for years and stuffed my face, doubling my body weight from eight and a half stone to a whopping sixteen and a half stone. My self-esteem hit rock bottom and most days I felt so depressed about my body, I couldn't bear to leave the house. I was no longer 'Claire from Steps'; I was the 'fat one from Steps'.

It's taken a long time, but I've finally got my diet demons under control. Now when I look in the mirror I'm drawn more to the positives than the negatives. I don't think I'll ever be completely happy with the way I look – what woman is? But I've finally realized I don't have to be skinny to be attractive and that I can look good at a size 14.

By getting up on stage again I want to prove to myself that I don't have to be a bag of bones to do this job and that, ultimately, the reason I'm here is because of my voice – not the size of my bum! I want to do it for every single woman who has tweeted or emailed me to say they've been held back because of their size.

So much has happened in my life since I joined Steps – some of it good, some of it bad – but it's all helped to make me a much stronger person. And this time around I know it's going to be different because I'm happy.

In the audience tonight will be my gorgeous husband, who's stuck by me through thick and thin (literally!), and my two beautiful children. Their love and support has given me the confidence and self-belief to get back on that stage and, when the performance is over and the lights go down, I know I'll be going home to our lovely family life.

'Two minutes, guys!' shouts our tour manager. Oh, my God, this is it now!

My friend and make-up artist Jackie swoops in for a final touch up. 'Right, you're all set, Claire. Good luck!' she says, squeezing my arm.

As I look round at the rest of the band, everyone is grinning from ear to ear and buzzing with excitement. It's time to get into position. We're about to make a spectacular entrance, coming up through the stage in Perspex tubes through a mist of dry ice, as if we've been cryogenically frozen for the past ten years!

As the intro music for our song 'Here & Now' starts, the audience cheers and I'm genuinely overwhelmed that our amazing fans still want to come and see us after all this time away. It feels just like it did back in 1997, waiting in the wings before our first big show, desperate to give the performance of our lives.

I've been given a second chance to live my dream and it's the best feeling in the world. I'm back, doing what I love most – and this time I'm going to have fun!

1

THE SINDY SWINGERS

I like to think I was always destined to be a singer because I was born on the day Elvis died. When I made my entrance into the world at 1.30 a.m. on 17 August 1977, it was still the 16th in Memphis, the day Elvis passed away. My mum told me there was a terrible thunderstorm raging while she was in labour and, growing up, I used to imagine it was the gods bringing Elvis's spirit to me! When the newspapers were delivered on the morning of the 17th, the front-page headlines all screamed out 'The King is dead!' So while my mum was ecstatically happy with her new bundle of joy, all the nurses were wandering around weeping because Elvis Presley had left the building for the final time. Call me stupid or crazy (a few have), but when I was a teenager I liked to imagine I was Elvis reincarnated.

I started my first pop band, The Sindy Swingers, at the grand old age of four. Also in the line-up were my best friend Melanie Huse, her little sister Hayley and my younger sister

Gemma. We were all obsessed with Sindy dolls, hence the band name, which was given to us by Mel's dad. We spent many afternoons at each other's houses, singing our favourite nursery rhymes or whatever happened to be in the charts at the time, while bashing away on a toy keyboard and drums.

As kids, Melanie and I were similar in every way apart from looks – she had brown, slightly wild curly hair, while mine was blonde and poker straight with a fringe. She was easy-going just like I was and we had loads of fun growing up. I've known her my whole life and now, even if we haven't seen each other for months, when we do get together we can pick up exactly where we left off. Thirty years on, we still try to meet up with Gemma and Hayley once a year for a Sindy Swingers reunion, although we're usually sipping cocktails at the Dorchester rather than performing a dodgy version of 'Message In A Bottle' in my mum's front room!

Despite the fact that I wasn't on vocals – I played recorder in the band – my mum says I was singing before I could talk. Dad had a friend at work who was a huge Police fan and she'd make tapes for us. Apparently I could sit for hours singing along to 'Roxanne' over and over again, which must have been delightful for my parents.

I'd put on little shows for them all the time. I had a wooden desk and a stool that went with it, and I'd plonk them both in the living room as props and say, 'Right, I'm doing a show now,' and then I'd belt out 'Over The Rainbow' from *The Wizard Of Oz*, 'Feed The Birds' from *Mary Poppins* and 'The Sun Will Come Out Tomorrow' from *Annie*.

We had a battered old suitcase full of dressing-up clothes and I'd do a costume change for every single song, sneaking behind the sofa to swap my outfit. One year, when we were getting our living room decorated, my Uncle John even drew a set on the wall behind me.

I was born at Hillingdon Hospital in Uxbridge, Middlesex, as were my sister Gemma (who's sixteen months younger than I am), my parents Bob and Nina, and both my children. And I haven't moved very far since – I still live just five minutes down the road.

I've never been a rebellious person or a risk-taker – maybe it's because I'm the eldest and I have that sense of responsibility of not upsetting my parents! They met when my mum, Nina, was only sixteen and my dad, Bob, was twenty-two, and married four years later, although I didn't come along for another four years after that.

Dad is very laidback and easy-going – it takes a lot to make him angry and I'm similar to him in that way. But he's a bit of a perfectionist, so everything's got to be in its place. He's slim and an inch shorter than me at 5ft 5in, and he's got no hair on top, which he'll kill me for saying! He's always had a moustache – he got rid of it once, but Gemma and I freaked out so he never shaved it off again.

Mum is a petite blonde who's a bit more fiery than Dad and quite outspoken – in fact, she doesn't take any crap from anyone! She loves me and my sister fiercely and has always been very protective of us: if there was ever a problem with me or Gemma at school, she'd be straight up there to sort it out. She's also very well turned out – whether she's going out for the night or just to work, she always makes an effort to dress smartly.

For as long as I can remember Mum worked for Xerox, although she always told them she couldn't work during the school holidays because she had to look after us (I think she was still using that excuse when we were eighteen!). And Dad has always worked in air and sea freight, and set up his own business years ago. Originally he had a partner, but eventually he took over the business and just had a PA working for him.

He used to work late every Friday, so Mum's sister Heather would come over and we'd have fish and chips or cauliflower cheese with bread and butter for tea, which I loved! It was a real treat. Sometimes Dad would have to work on a Saturday and he'd take me and Gemma with him. I loved poking around his office until I stapled my finger.

Gemma and I were really close growing up, and still are. We're the same height and both blonde, but she's always been petite like Mum and Dad. She can have a bit of a temper, but she's very funny and lots of fun to be around. We used to gang up on my mum sometimes for a laugh. Mum's deaf in one ear and whenever we were out shopping she'd never answer when we shouted 'Mum!', only when we shouted 'Nina!', so we'd always call her Nina when we were mucking around.

We had a lovely, happy childhood and were quite sheltered – nothing really bad ever happened and there was never a crisis at home. So it came as a shock when things started to go horribly wrong for me in my twenties, and I remember thinking at the time, 'The reason bad things are happening now is because I had everything growing up and was so lucky for such a long time.'

I can remember our first house in Lees Road like we lived there only yesterday. It was a modern end-of-terrace house that had an alley running up the side leading to Melanie's house, which was identical to ours. There was a little porch and when you walked into our living room it had brown swirly carpet and a massive wall-to-wall fireplace that looked like it was made out of paving stones – all very seventies! But it was a real fire and we all loved it.

We also had a nice little garden out the back, although for years my dad parked his speedboat there (he never used it, but had to have it nonetheless!). The boat made a great place for us to play, though.

We'd go abroad for our summer holiday every year, although there were a couple of years when Dad's business wasn't doing so well and we couldn't afford it. We went to Malta and to Disney World in Florida, and we had a few caravan holidays in Spain and France with my mum's older sister, Cheryl, her husband John, and their kids Jason and Justin.

Growing up we did so much together as a family – every evening Gemma and I would sit at the table to have our dinner with Mum and Dad. I always loved food and was never a fussy eater. Mum says when we went to a Chinese restaurant they'd give me a spring roll and I'd chew on it happily for hours.

Perhaps unsurprisingly, given that I was to become Britain's most famous yo-yo dieter, some of my earliest memories involve food. When I was really little, Mum took me to tap and ballet, but there was one problem – the biscuit break came at the end of the two classes and I wanted it to be in between. When Mum explained they weren't going to change this just for me I remember saying to her, 'I don't like ballet, Mum. I don't want to go any more.' I was clearly only interested if I got a treat at half time!

Spaghetti Bolognese was my favourite meal of all until I was about four years old and I'd eaten a big plate of it for my tea. Afterwards, I went into the living room and started jumping from the coffee table to the sofa, as children do, except I slipped, knocking myself out and giving myself concussion, which made me sick. From that day on, I never ate another plate of the stuff again.

Burgers and baked beans always remind me of being a kid. We used to visit Auntie Cheryl and Uncle John in Oxfordshire – he's originally from Kentucky in the US – and he'd cook burgers, barbecue ribs and BBQ beans, which I adored. Then we'd have pancakes for breakfast with crispy bacon and eggs, and pour maple syrup all over it. Delicious!

Visiting my granddad – Laurie – on my dad's side was a treat, too. He always had Mr Kipling Country Slices that had big lumps of crunchy sugar on top and I'd sneak into the larder to steal one when the adults were all chatting in the living room. I'm sure if I'd asked I'd have been allowed to have one!

It seems I always had my eye on how to bag myself some goodies. When I was still at infant school, I had a teacher called Mrs Green who was diabetic and always had Club biscuits in her drawer.

'Mrs Green, I'm really hungry because Mummy didn't make me any breakfast,' I said to her one morning, putting on the saddest look I could manage.

'You poor thing,' she said, giving me one of her Clubs. My plan had worked! I sneakily turned my back to the rest of the class to eat it.

To think up that story at the age of five just to get some chocolate is pretty calculating and I'm horrified now to think I deprived that poor woman of her biscuit. It's one story I'm not so proud of! I got my comeuppance though: we were all standing outside the school gates at home time with our mums when one of my classmates piped up, 'Claire told Mrs Green she didn't have any breakfast and she gave her a biscuit.' My mum was mortified and I was whisked off home and sent to my room!

At home, Mum only ever allowed us to have fizzy drinks and chocolate on special occasions such as Christmas, so I used to love going to Melanie's house because they had big tubs of ice cream and proper chocolate bars. Even if my dad had a big bar of chocolate at Christmas, he'd break off one square, wrap it back up and put it in the fridge, taking a little bit every now and then. Given the chance, I'd have scoffed the entire thing in one go, but instead I'd steal little bits of it from the fridge.

Mum always encouraged us to eat healthy, wholesome meals like homemade shepherd's pie or lasagne, and there was always plenty of veg on the side. I certainly had a big, healthy appetite from an early age, unlike my sister Gemma, who was always sitting at the table fiddling with her food ages after I'd scoffed mine and left. We were always told we should clear our plates before getting down from the table, so that's what I used to do – with glee! I'd eat the lot, even if I felt full up, because I hated getting told off for anything.

I remember visiting my Auntie Chris, who had a grand townhouse in Islington, and she'd dish up huge, man-sized portions of food. I'd eat the lot and still have pudding afterwards. But I never remember feeling bad about it or being sick because I'd eaten too much. And I was a healthy, normal weight, so at that stage food was never an issue.

When I was at junior school, I developed a passion for baking and I still love it to this day. Every Saturday I'd get my mum's cookbook out and bake as many things as I could: fruitcake, shortbread and scones. I'd put all the ingredients in separate bowls and pretend I was on a cooking show. I baked Eccles cakes once and made the flaky pastry from scratch. I wanted to be a pastry chef for a while until I found out how much training and hard work was involved!

Strangely enough, I was never really interested in eating what I'd baked; it was more about pleasing other people and getting praise for my efforts. I felt so proud when people said my cakes were amazing, and I still love it when friends enjoy what I've baked.

My other passion – apart from food – was, of course, singing. When I was about ten and still at Hillingdon Primary, I signed up for a summer project at the Beck Theatre in Hayes. I got to perform in the chorus of *The Wizard Of Oz* and *Alice In Wonderland*, and I'd go to rehearsals every day, then do a couple of nights in the show. It was my first experience of performing for a proper audience and I had fun doing it.

Mel and I were also huge fans of the R&B group Five Star and we wrote to *Jim'll Fix It* several times, asking to meet them. Sadly, we never got a reply! But we did put together a little show for the school assembly with our tribute band Five Star Plus One (because there were six of us) *and* we performed a dance routine and little comedy sketches. I played a character called Mrs Cookery, who was a bit like the Swedish Chef from *The Muppet Show*. It was probably absolutely diabolical so let's hope no one filmed it.

The summer before I started secondary school was the first time I remember being a bit chubby, but around then I started going to a running club three times a week with my friend Louise. Her dad, Ron, who was a friend of my dad, knew the guy who ran the club and I think they saw it as an opportunity for us to get involved in sport. It was good for me in other ways, too. I was a painfully shy child and would clam up if I didn't know people, so the club put me in a situation where I had to interact with other kids and make friends. I absolutely hated taking part in competitions, though, because I was rubbish. Every competition involved a long-distance race, a sprint and a field event like throwing the discus. Every time I did the long distance, I'd be way out in front, but by the end of the race you could guarantee that every other person had lapped me and I'd limp in last. But when I got to secondary school I enjoyed playing netball and hockey, so although I was never skinny – I was born with chunky thighs – I was slim and quite athletic.

Although I went on to be plagued by insecurities about my body when I was in Steps, I never remember worrying about my figure as a child, even though a few of the kids called me tree-trunk legs! I was more bothered about my spots, which I tried to cover up with a fringe that I scrunched up with loads of hairspray.

That first year at Bishopshalt School was when I discovered The Carpenters. I saw the TV movie *The Karen Carpenter Story* in 1989 and instantly fell in love with the music. I couldn't believe my luck when I realized Mum had the *Ticket To Ride* album, and I started playing it constantly in my bedroom.

It was Karen's voice more than anything that moved me – it was just so beautiful. Before I'd heard The Carpenters I used to belt out songs at the top of my voice, but listening to Karen and trying to copy how she sang is really how I learnt to do it properly. She put so much emotion into it, and you believe every single word she sings.

Although I was only eleven years old, I was captivated by her story and so sad when I learnt she'd died at just thirty-two from heart failure as a result of anorexia. I don't think I even knew what anorexia was then, but I remembered the word and, years later, I was to understand only too well what it meant.

According to reports, Karen's illness was triggered by a comment in a newspaper about Richard Carpenter and his 'chubby sister', and I think it got to her. She was only a teenager, after all. I know now that when you're young and in the spotlight and feel under pressure – not only to perform but to look a certain way – controlling your food intake gives you the sense you're in control of your life.

I also read that when on stage, Karen always wanted to hide behind the drums but she was forced to get out front and sing, even though she didn't want to – she liked the comfort of having the drum kit around her. It reminded me of when I was little and was asked to sing at family get-togethers. I'd either hide behind the sofa or the curtains so no one could see me, and they'd all be straining to listen. I don't know why I did that because there was no pressure back then, but while I didn't mind singing in front of Mum and Dad, my inherent lack of self-confidence and shyness came out when I was asked to perform on my own and be the focus of everyone's attention. I've always worried about being good enough and I've always wanted to please other people and win their approval – even if it's just from baking a birthday cake. I've never been able to bear the thought of someone not liking me.

I definitely have The Carpenters to thank for getting my voice noticed. At Bishopshalt we had to do a practical music exam so I got a book of Carpenters sheet music and sang 'Goodbye To Love'. I got 99 per cent!

I was walking down the corridor at school one day when my music teacher Mr King came over.

'Do you realize how good a singer you are, Claire?' he said.

'Er, I like it,' I mumbled shyly, 'and I like singing to The Carpenters.'

'Well, I want you to sing in assembly next week.'

'Oh, er . . .' I stammered.

He hurried off before I had a chance to say no, leaving me standing there in shock. Then I started crying. I was a bit overwhelmed – I felt proud of myself for being asked, but was terrified by the thought of performing in front of the whole school. On the day my singing was OK but probably not perfect as I was so nervous!

I think most kids have a teacher who's a big influence, and Mr King turned out to be an important person in my life. He was a big guy with a rugby player's physique and could be quite stern, but he was really kind, too. If it hadn't been for him, I don't think I would ever have been able to build up the confidence to sing solo in front of that many people. He did push me, but it was all for my benefit because he genuinely thought I had potential. If someone in authority tells me to do something, I tend not to argue and, in this case, I'm glad I didn't.

My mum always used to say I had a great voice, but I think you're more likely to believe praise when it comes from outside your family. I was twelve years old at the time and Mum asked me if I wanted to go to a stage school, but I didn't want to go. I imagined everyone who went to stage school was like Bonnie Langford and I just didn't think I'd fit in or have the confidence to make new friends. But from then on, Mr King used to take me out with the school orchestra to sing at local junior schools.

Every year, too, there was a Christmas show for the upper school and when I was in the third year, they invited me to audition: I think Mr King was keen for me to get as much experience as possible. So I was in the chorus of *Babes in Arms* and the following year I was in the chorus of *Guys and Dolls*.

Of course there were other distractions at school – the usual things every young girl goes through, like being completely tormented because you're in love with some boy who doesn't love you back. I had my first big crush when I was eleven, on Douglas Fowler, who was in the same year as me at school. I ended up going out with him on and off until we were seventeen. I'm sure it all started with a 'Will you get off with me?' moment, but I think I was too scared! I did pluck up the courage in the end, though, and he was the first boy I kissed.

Doug was really popular – clever, funny and brilliant at sport. And he had red hair, although he always used to insist it was strawberry blond! I was so in love with him and, until I got out into the big wide world, I was convinced we were going to get married. We never slept together, though – our relationship was very innocent and involved nothing more than kissing, really.

For our first proper date we went to the cinema to see *The Bodyguard* with Whitney Houston. It was freezing, so he lent me one of his gloves: only the one, mind! Usually, he'd just come over to my house – we'd moved by then to a bungalow with a loft conversion on Micawber Avenue, and there was a TV room upstairs. So Doug and I would sit up there and watch telly. I don't even remember talking that much – we'd watch telly, have a snog and then he'd go home.

I always thought he looked like Rick Astley and I was obsessed with Rick at the time; I even had a poster of him next to my bed. Years later, quite soon after I'd joined Steps, I met him at PWL, Pete Waterman's recording studio in London. H and I were punching each other with excitement, screeching, 'Look, it's Rick Astley!' I was standing at the reception desk thinking I was going to pass out because Rick was right in front of me!

'Um, nice to meet you,' was all I managed to get out, while I gazed at my teenage crush in awe.

He said something polite in return, and then we all ordered a Chinese takeaway and sat down together to eat it. These days I'd be tweeting about that!

When I was about fourteen I also had a huge crush on every member of Take That. Melanie and I would go to our school friend Hayley Pile's house every lunchtime without fail, and she'd cook frozen pizza while we watched Take That videos. I was convinced I was the female Gary Barlow: whenever I'd sing Take That records I'd think, 'Oh, I sound like Gary Barlow!'

Around this time I started stewarding at Wembley Arena, which I did for a few years. There was a boy I went to school with who had asked if I fancied coming along and doing it with him. It involved showing the audience to their seats, then walking up and down during the performance to make sure people weren't standing on the chairs or generally misbehaving. We got paid £10 for the night and most times you'd get to see the band. I used to bunk off school a bit early to get there for 4 p.m. as that way you'd get a good slot and wouldn't be stuck up in the top tier of the arena.

I always made sure I was working when Take That were on. Seeing my idols perform was such a thrill and it was really the only reason I did the job because the money was rubbish! Years later, when Steps performed at the Brit Awards for the first time in 1998, we were walking back to our table and Mark Owen shouted over, 'It's Steps!' I thought I was going to have a heart attack brought on by pure excitement!

'Mark Owen knows who we are! I've made it!' I thought. If I hadn't had really bad tonsillitis I think I would have made the most of it.

I was a big Prince fan, too, and I stewarded about nine Wembleys with him. You were never allowed to watch the sound check or even to stand and watch the show, so I used to walk up and down the aisles all the time and whenever I was walking towards the stage I'd make sure it was really, really slowly so I could see Prince.

I used to gaze up at that stage and daydream of singing on it one day, but not in a million years did I think I'd actually be standing up there just a few years later with my own band, performing to thousands of screaming fans.

One night when I was working there, a guy came over to me and gave me his card. He was from a model agency and told me to call if I was interested. I was flattered that someone thought I could be a model, so when I got home I showed the card to my mum.

'Hmm, I'm not sure about this,' she said, turning the card over in her hand.

'Go on, just ring the number. You never know,' I urged.

Mum called the next day and a woman answered.

'Someone gave your card to my daughter, but she's only fifteen,' said my mum.

'Well, we only work for the best publications,' the woman replied defensively. 'You know – *Mayfair*, *Penthouse* . . .'

'Er, she's not interested and she never will be!' snapped my mum before hanging up.

I was mortified! It was a glamour model agency.

★

I was fifteen when I first thought about the possibility of making a career out of performing. Mr King asked me to audition for the lead role in the Christmas show that year. The part was Maria in *The Sound Of Music* and I got it.

That performance was a light bulb moment for me, and it felt like a huge step because the success of the show hinged on my part. It opens with Maria singing 'The Sound Of Music', and I was quaking with fear in my nun's habit when it was time to go on stage. I'd only ever sung in the chorus at the Christmas show, so this felt like a very big deal.

The set was pretty basic – just a painted backdrop of a mountain and the odd prop here and there. I started off standing on some stairs so it would look like I was on the mountain, then the curtains opened and I launched into 'The hills are alive with the sound of music', giving it everything I had. Singing was what I loved more than anything else in the world – suddenly my nerves disappeared and it just felt so right.

There were loads of costume changes and our lovely Home Economics teacher, Mrs Bull, had made all the outfits. Maria marries Von Trapp in the production so I got to wear my first wedding dress! For that part of the show I had to walk down the aisle through the audience and I'll never forget seeing Mum and Dad, both of whom had an 'Oh my God!' look of shock on their faces. I was holding fake calla lilies and at that moment, I thought, 'I'm living my dream!'

I loved the applause, the flowers and the congratulations – I was hooked. Even now, if I'm out shopping in

Uxbridge, mums and dads who had kids at the school when I was there still congratulate me on my performance in *The Sound Of Music*. They'll say things like, 'Oh, remember when you were Maria? You were great!'

I think I did all right, considering I'd never been to stage school and had given up on dance classes when I was about three or four but, up until that point, although I knew I had a big voice, I never thought I was any good. I've always felt a bit uncomfortable accepting praise, even though I'm always seeking it! When it comes to the way I look, or my voice, I just have trouble believing the nice things that people say.

The following year I was Nancy in *Oliver!*, but the year after that I had to focus on exams, so I wasn't allowed to go for a lead part and ended up playing a prostitute in *Cabaret*. I wasn't thrilled about that – my costume was a skimpy teddy belonging to my mum, which exposed my thighs to the entire school. Very embarrassing!

I always liked the social side of secondary school, but not the academic part. My concentration isn't great, so I used to chat all the time and was always getting told off for talking; all my school reports said, 'Claire should talk less.' By the end of every lesson, my friends would have finished their work, even though they'd been talking too, but I never seemed to get everything done. And I hated getting up early! I was supposed to walk to school, but I'd be running late pretty much every day and my dad would have to take me in. I didn't mind, though, because he drove a Jag, so I felt like the bee's knees pulling up at the school gates in that.

If I'd put my mind to schoolwork I think I would have done better because I'm not stupid, but I didn't apply myself at all. Although it was pretty obvious I was never going to be a scientist or a mathematician, I did well enough in my GCSEs to stay on at school to do A-levels in Sports Science and English. At one point, I even thought about going to Loughborough University to train to be a PE teacher. I guess if I'd taken that road, I wouldn't have got fat! Luckily, I'd also been developing my singing, which ultimately saved me from a lifetime of hanging around freezing-cold hockey pitches.

Although being asked to sing at assembly and performing in the Christmas shows was a brilliant opportunity, it also got me the wrong kind of attention from some girls at school and sparked a bit of jealousy, which I wasn't prepared for.

Nasty things started being said about me behind my back after I sang that first time during assembly – I remember a few girls talking about it afterwards, saying, 'I don't know what the fuss is about. She isn't that good a singer'. Or I'd overhear snide comments like, 'Claire really loves herself', or 'She's such a snobby cow'. I don't know why they said those things, because I never behaved like I thought I was someone special. In fact, I used to stand there in assembly in front of everyone absolutely crapping myself. I never moved, I never really smiled and then I'd quickly return to my seat as soon as I'd finished the song.

One day after school, Gemma and I were walking towards

Coney Green, which was a shortcut home, when we turned the corner and saw that practically everyone from school was on the field. This usually meant there was going to be a fight. We spotted two of my friends – Natasha Claxton and Suzanne Greaves – and they shouted, 'Claire! They're all waiting for you! You should go the other way. Debbie's going to beat you up!'

Debbie, who now works in a local shop, was one of the tough girls at school. My blood turned to ice and I quickly spun around and walked the other way. Any kind of confrontation is my absolute worst nightmare – I can't even have an argument with someone without crying. There was no way I was going to stand and face her, but all the way home two boys were chasing me on their bikes shouting, 'Go on, Claire, you can have her, you can have her!' I was shaking with fear by the time I got home.

My mum went straight up to the school and Debbie never gave me any trouble after that, but a few similar things happened. One of my friends was going out with a boy who was a couple of years above us and, because of that, and the fact that I knew some of the older boys from the Christmas shows, a lot of the older girls hated me. I was walking across the field on Tog Day (when we didn't have to wear our uniform) feeling happy in my flared jeans and flowy hippy top, and one of the boys said something to me. Before I could reply, one of the older girls screeched, 'What are you fucking talking to her for? Do you think she's pretty?' Again, I just took off and started running home.

I was popular in my year because I wasn't naughty, and I had a talent I suppose, but everyone else – especially the older girls – thought I was stuck up and big-headed. But really I was just shy: when I walked through the corridors at school I'd keep my head down and just go to where I had to be. So maybe because I didn't smile and chat to people I didn't know, I got a bit of a reputation for being a snob.

I never understood, though, why those girls would be jealous of me. I might have envied other girls for certain things – because they had skinny legs or a hot boyfriend – but it was never to the point of being nasty. As far as the singing went, I was doing it because Mr King asked me to do it. I loved to sing, of course, but I also found it a completely terrifying experience and I'd panic every time I had to perform, so I was never pushy or arrogant when it came to my ability. But I didn't say anything back when I heard those nasty comments, so I suppose I fuelled those feelings by not standing up for myself.

Something similar was to happen years later in Steps.

Maybe if I had walked across that field and got beaten up, my life would have taken a totally different path. I might have given up on my dreams. Instead, I was never harmed physically by the older girls at school – it was more verbal bullying, which still hurt and felt threatening. But somehow I found the courage to go on and make a career out of singing.

2

NOT SO MYSTERIOUS GIRL

'The Heath Tavern on the Uxbridge Road has a karaoke competition on Sundays. Do you fancy going?' asked Mel.

'We can't!' I said, shocked. We were probably not quite seventeen yet and still at school, so not old enough to be going to a pub.

'Come on, we won't drink; we'll just have a Coke,' she said. 'Let's go.'

The Tavern was run by an Irish family, and I suppose the best way to describe it would be as an old man's pub. The first time I went there it was dead, but there was a tiny stage in one corner with a little karaoke machine perched on top of it. I was with Melanie and Hayley Pile, and Mel and I sang 'I Wanna Dance With Somebody'.

After that, we started going every Sunday and it was such a laugh. It wasn't long before word spread and more and more people from school came along, so it got to the point where it became absolutely rammed when finals night came around, every couple of months.

I never did Carpenters songs at those competitions; always big power ballads so everyone would think, 'Whoa!' I started winning the Tavern competitions and the prize money of £100, usually with 'I Will Always Love You' or 'Greatest Love Of All' – there was a lot of Whitney in my repertoire.

I remember a few girls saying, 'I don't know why she keeps winning, I'm better than her!' There was one girl in particular called Naomi, who was my equivalent from another school, and there was a bit of competition about who was the better singer.

After I won three times, I was entered into the inter-brewery competition and I won that as well, but this time the prize was a trip to New York. I didn't want the trip, though, so I asked if I could have the cash instead, which must have been at least £500!

Unfortunately, I was barred from entering the competitions from then on because I kept winning, but they said I could be a judge. It meant I got free drinks all night, but had to sit by myself in the corner. As annoyed as I was that they'd barred me, it was nice to think I'd found something I could be the best at. Looking back, those karaoke years were brilliant – even now I love thinking, 'They barred me because no one could beat me!'

After that, I started entering little talent competitions in clubs and pubs, which I never won: the bloody comedian or the magician always got first prize. My mum and Auntie Chris would try to come along to all of those shows and when I didn't get through to the next round they'd be absolutely outraged.

'I can't believe it! I can't believe it!' Auntie Chris would shout.

'She sings that better than Whitney!' Mum would chime in.

'Um, no, I don't, but thanks anyway, Mum!' I'd mutter.

On a few occasions I remember looking out into the audience and my mum and all my aunties – Chris, Pauline, Cheryl and Heather – would be singing along, using their hairbrushes or bingo pens as mics; they sang into whatever they could find in their handbags. Dad, on the other hand, was never able to cope that well with watching me sing as he'd get too nervous. When I won the New York trip, I actually thought he was going to have a heart attack because he was constantly pacing up and down! Even later, when I was performing in Steps, he couldn't handle it, although when I took part in *Popstar To Operastar* in 2011, he would have come down to the studio every week if he'd been offered seats. He's got bragging rights now!

Once we went to someone's family do where there was karaoke and, after I sang, the guy running it, who was called Woody, came over to speak to me.

'You're a really good singer,' he said. 'I'm running a Karaoke competition next week; do you fancy coming along to sing?'

He was the first person I met who promised he could do all sorts to help launch my singing career, including getting me a record deal. You soon realize there are quite a lot of those characters around, but I was seventeen and pretty naïve, so I believed him. Nothing ever materialized of course.

The talent competition was at a hall in Reading and a whole coachload of friends and family came down to watch me. I sang 'Flashdance' and 'The Greatest Love of All', and I won. The prize was a short recording session in Woody's 'studio', which was actually a shed in his back yard.

Nevertheless, it was a chance to record something and I chose 'Evergreen' and 'I Will Always Love You'. I'm sure I still have a tape of it somewhere!

I left school in the summer of 1995, a couple of months before my eighteenth birthday. By then I was single again. Douglas was going off to university in America and I had decided there was no point in us continuing to see each other. Although it was me who pushed for us to split up I was still upset about it and, when I waved him off at the bus station on the day of his flight, the tears were streaming down my face. I'd well up every time I heard Joni Mitchell's 'Big Yellow Taxi', which was our song – someone had done a cover version of it and it was played on the radio all the time.

I decided to take the whole summer off to decide what I wanted to do: I hadn't applied to university. Deep down, I hoped I could make a career out of singing – after all, I'd been winning competitions and people were telling me I was good at it. Most people anyway! I told the head of sixth form that I'd applied to stage school to get out of explaining why I wasn't going to university, and he said to me in an extremely condescending tone: 'Claire, you do realize you have to be extremely talented to get into stage school, don't you?'

I just thought, 'Right, OK, you cheeky bastard, I'll show you!'

My mum and dad wouldn't have let me sit around doing nothing all summer, though. They had always drummed into me the importance of getting a job to pay your way, and I liked to have my own money, too. Gemma and I were never deprived, but we weren't spoilt kids, either, although at Christmas and birthdays we'd pretty much always get what we wanted. One year I asked for a keyboard with a drum machine on it. Up until Christmas Eve my parents were saying, 'You're not getting it,' then my dad buckled and said, 'Oh, come on then, let's go and get it.' But the rest of the year we didn't get expensive presents and, if we wanted something, we'd have to pay for it ourselves.

I got my first Saturday job in a florist shop just up the road from the Heath Tavern, when I was eleven. I'd never worked in a florist before and I was making up bouquets and working a twelve-hour day for £10, so Mum went crazy and rang them to say I wasn't going back! Then I worked in a greengrocer's. I wasn't allowed in the shop, but I used to sit out the back making up fruit baskets for the airlines.

I had to be there for 8.30 every Saturday morning and I got paid £12.75. I did that for about a year and a half until I got a job in a fabric shop, which paid really well: £35 for the day and they doubled that at Christmas!

I saved up the money I earned in that job to pay for the insurance on my first car – a maroon Renault 5 Campus that Mum and Dad bought from some neighbours up the road. It was a present for my seventeenth birthday and although it had a tiny engine and would make a right racket in the wind, I loved that car and kept it immaculate. In fact, I still had it when I first got into Steps and I'd drive us all over the place in it. I remember driving from Epsom in Surrey, where we were rehearsing, to our record company in Willesden in north-west London where we were doing a showcase for Pete Waterman. H and Faye were with me and we sang at the tops of our voices all the way there!

I was still working in the fabric shop the summer I left school so I could earn money while pondering my future. I was singing in competitions whenever I could and, one night at karaoke, I met a girl called Joanne who said she used to have a recording deal and that she could introduce me to people.

She took me to meet this guy, Terry Adams, at his recording studio near Shepperton. I was impressed because it had a proper mixing desk – a big improvement on Woody's garden shed. Terry was a record producer, although he was still very young. Also there were Ben from Curiosity Killed

The Cat and another guy called Paul Fitzgerald. Nothing came of the meeting, but that same summer, Joanne, who I'd become friendly with, started going out with Terry and we were invited to a birthday party for one of his friends. Paul was there, too, and I got talking to him about singing. He had the patter and was really friendly – a bit of a cheeky chappy, I suppose.

When we were leaving he said, 'Look, I'm an agent and I'm working with a record company that's talking about putting a girl band together. Are you interested?'

'Of course!' I replied straightaway.

'OK, ring me on Monday and I'll give you the details,' he replied, passing me his business card.

The party was on the Saturday night and on the following Monday, as promised, Paul gave me the number of a guy at the record company called Phil France. He asked me to come up that very day, so I grabbed Mum and off we went to their offices in Soho Square, London.

The company was called Avex, a Japanese label that was trying to establish itself in the UK. Phil came out to greet us and we sat at a meeting table in the open-plan offices to chat about the band and the two other girls who were already in it. Phil seemed very sure of himself and quite flippant about things.

'Bonnie, yeah, she's gorgeous. She's got an amazing body and she's a brilliant dancer,' he said. 'And Cossie . . . she's also got an amazing body and a great voice.'

'Right, OK then,' I thought. I wasn't quite sure how to

reply to that! I wasn't even asked to sing: Phil just said, 'Do you wanna do it, then?'

I was fresh out of school with no experience of the music business, so immediately I said, 'Uh, yeah!'

I couldn't believe they hadn't even bothered to audition me.

I was sent off to a recording studio in Fulham to try to record a track with a guy whose name was Boris. It was called 'Heart & Soul' and I sang it really nicely, but at the end Boris just said, 'If you want to do this, Claire, you're going to have to rough up your voice a bit and drop your Ts and Hs.'

Because I was quite well-spoken and I sang so much West End musical stuff, my words were quite pronounced and my style just wasn't raw enough. So, with a promise to 'rough up' my voice, I signed the deal to become part of girl band TSD with Bonnie and Cossie on my eighteenth birthday. Paul was also hired by the record company to manage us.

I'm often asked what TSD stands for and the answer is nothing really. The Japanese executives wanted us to be called The Scan Dolls, but Phil didn't think that would work for the UK market, so he shortened it. Later, we used to tell people it stood for Three Strapping Dykes! The official story was that we put our hands into a bag of Scrabble letters and picked out TSD.

I met Cossie and Bonnie for the first time at a lunch

organized by the record company. I hit it off with Cossie immediately: we were very similar in personality and liked a lot of the same things. She was quite small and pretty with long dark hair and blonde highlights. Everyone liked her – she was bubbly and good fun, and really softly spoken. She'd been to the Sylvia Young Theatre School in west London with Denise Van Outen and Melanie Blatt from All Saints.

I liked Bonnie at that first meeting too, although it soon became apparent that she was a real party girl and we didn't have much in common at all. Her look was quite different to Cossie's – she was blonde at the time, with big boobs, long skinny legs and big pouty lips.

We had a laugh at the lunch and when we left the restaurant, the three of us linked arms and skipped off down the street, laughing and chatting, very excited about what the future held.

We got paid £1,000 a month and because I still lived at home with Mum and Dad and I was on tour the rest of the time, I felt pretty rich. I started to spend all my money on clothes – what teenage girl wouldn't? But I always had an eye for a bargain and loved Gordons Connections down the road in Yiewsley, because it had high street brands at really cheap prices. I bought a black satin fishtail French Connection skirt in there once for £11, which I ended up wearing to the MTV awards in Dublin with Steps a couple of years later!

*

Almost as soon as we signed our deal, the record company enlisted the help of a choreographer who put all three of us on a diet. She was a ballet dancer and had a really skinny, toned body, and hair that was scraped back into a bun.

I don't actually know how much I weighed then because I never used scales, but I was no more than a size 10 or 12. I was always aware that I had a big bum and used to try to hide it by tying jumpers and sweatshirts around my waist, which probably made me look even bigger. But I was always tiny up top with a slim waist and small boobs.

Cossie was about three inches shorter than me, but had exactly the same body shape – no boobs and a big bum! Bonnie couldn't dance to save her life, despite what Phil France had said, and she couldn't sing either, so she was obviously in the band for another reason. She had the boobs and the legs, but she had a bit of a tummy, too.

We all had to stick to a really strict diet, which meant we could only eat 1,000 calories a day (half the number of daily calories recommended for a woman). It was basically turkey and peas, and we were allowed to eat fish fingers and beans, too, but I don't remember finding it all that hard.

If I'm being honest, I probably wasn't even making it to 1,000 calories a day because I was working out a lot, too. When we rehearsed at Pineapple Dance Studios, they used to do a little fruit salad in a cup with yogurt on top and I'd have that every day.

For dance training and the gym I used to put on trousers that ballet dancers wear to make them sweat and lose water

– I picked up that tip from our choreographer. Imagine a pair of waders made out of bin bags and you get the picture! Underneath those I'd wear this big waistband I bought from Argos that also makes you sweat. On top of that lot was my workout gear.

At one point I was probably going to the gym every weekday but, despite the effort I was putting in, I don't remember getting that thin: they filmed a video of us and I still had a big bum and hips. I think it was because we didn't have a professional trainer helping us to do things properly so I'd just use the stairmaster all the time, which meant my thighs got even chunkier!

Being in TSD meant touring pretty much all the time – we did a *Smash Hits* arena tour, toured with Ant & Dec (although they were called PJ & Duncan at that time, the names of the characters they played in the TV show *Byker Grove*), Boyzone and again with Ant & Dec. I loved it because I'd gone from being a fan of these people to, 'Oh, my God, I'm on tour with them!'

Boyzone were massive at the time and we supported them after their breakthrough single 'Love Me For A Reason'. I was kind of awestruck and used to pinch myself because I couldn't believe I was meant to be in the same league as these bands we were supporting. But, while it was amazing to get the chance to sing in front of so many people, the audience wasn't really interested in us – they were always waiting for the main act to come on. We did start to build up our own little following, though.

We actually started out doing little Chart Invasion road-shows at weekends with Ant & Dec, Deuce (which had Ant McPartlin's now wife Lisa Armstrong in the line-up), Peter Andre, Ultimate Kaos, Boyzone, The Outhere Brothers, *EastEnders* actor-turned-singer Sean Maguire, and presenter Chris Rogers – best known for doing the BBC's *Newsround*. The gigs were often in local leisure centres; in fact, the first gig we did as TSD was in a sports hall in Torquay. I was so nervous, I knocked my mic off the stand.

We all stayed at the same hotels when we were doing the roadshows and would go to the bar for a drink after the gig and get up to all sorts of mischief! Back then there was a real sense of camaraderie and we had so much fun – the atmosphere was brilliant. It was a tradition on the last night of the tour to play pranks on each other and Sean Maguire and his tour manager – his cousin Mark – were usually involved somewhere along the line. Once they turned every single piece of furniture in Stephen Gately's room upside down after Boyzone hid some of the props for Sean's show. And I remember waking up one morning in Bournemouth to find that all our cars had been covered in eggs and toilet roll.

The Backstreet Boys supported Ant & Dec on the first tour. I decided they were really nice and everything, but they were never going to make it. The next thing I knew they were number one and only did half the tour! They were signed to Jive, which was the label that signed Steps two years later.

I had a massive crush on Kevin Richardson from the Backstreet Boys, who had dark hair and beautiful green eyes, and used to follow him around trying to talk to him. One day we were sitting together chatting and he said, 'You've got a really nice grill.' I didn't have a clue what he was talking about, although I found out later he meant my teeth! I was so close to him I probably could have snogged him, but I ran a mile instead and was devastated because he didn't look at me again after that.

I did, however, have a little tryst with Chris Rogers, who was blond and a few years older than me. He was the presenter on the Chart Invasion tours and we used to give him a lift in our van. He kept telling me I looked like Princess Di, although I think the only similarity was the blonde hair! At first we used to just have a laugh together, then he told our tour manager John Pryer that he fancied me and was going to propose to me! John thought it was funny and encouraged Chris to buy me a ring when he should have said, 'Don't do that, it's not a great idea. Maybe you should ask her out first,' like any normal person would have!

The two of them went out shopping and Chris bought me a ring – it wasn't a traditional engagement style but it was gold, and it had a tiny chip of a diamond in it. I walked into the dressing room one day and saw a teddy bear in the corner and a jewellery box next to it with the ring inside. I hadn't realized Chris liked me in that way – he hadn't even given me a peck on the cheek, let alone a proper kiss.

That night we all went to the bar and I said 'Thank you',

but there was a bit of a weird atmosphere so I went back to my room and called him to thank him again. He ended up coming up to my bedroom and we had a bit of a snog. We didn't do anything else – I told him I was a virgin and didn't want to have sex.

The next day I was off somewhere else with the band. I think I spoke to him on the phone after that, but then the Chart Invasion tours came to an end and that was that. I don't know to this day if it was a serious thing or not, but he still gave me the ring!

The whole thing was a bit embarrassing, to be honest. I was so young and didn't have much experience with boys; I didn't know how to cope with the attention. I was rubbish really. I hadn't had a boyfriend since splitting up with Doug. I'd been out on the odd date, but I'd always find a really stupid excuse not to go out with someone. Melanie once told me that a boy fancied me and I talked to him loads on the phone and even went on a date with him once, but decided not to take things further because I didn't like his puffa jacket. I didn't think it had enough stuffing in it – clearly a deal-breaker!

I had lots of little crushes when I was on tour with TSD – I fancied Dec Donnelly for a while, but I was far too scared to talk to him. I'd watched *Byker Grove* as a kid, so he seemed like a big star to me. I'd manage a 'Hello', then I'd clam up. He had a girlfriend, though, as did Ronan Keating, who I also had a thing for. I remember one day Cossie and I having lunch before playing at the Corn Exchange in Cambridge, sitting opposite Shane Lynch and Ronan, and their girlfriends Easther and Vernie, who were in Eternal. I'm sure the girls were giving me and Cossie evils in case we were looking at their men!

But my biggest crush of all was reserved for Peter Andre. He was in his early twenties and already pretty famous after his hit single 'Mysterious Girl'. I was completely and utterly obsessed with Pete – I LOVED him! On the Chart Invasion tours I'd hang around the corridors just in case he'd walk past and talk to me. His brother Danny looked after his security, so I'd always be saying to Danny, 'Can you just give Pete my number?' and 'Why doesn't he like me?'

I also talked to Pete's dancers all the time to try to get closer to him. I found out later that one of his dancers only talked to me because he fancied me himself – I ended up snogging him once, then never spoke to him again.

I must have driven people mad the way I used to go on about Pete. I genuinely thought I was in love, but all the people around him must have been thinking, 'For God's sake, please sort her out!' I was told that Pete knew I was still a virgin and that was why he didn't want to get involved with me. I guess he knew it wouldn't be a one-night stand kind of thing.

One night, though, we were in a hotel in Exeter and I bumped into him in the corridor.

'Come here,' he whispered in my ear, then took my hand and led me to the stairwell.

I've no idea if he said anything else after that because my heart was pounding so hard I could practically hear it, and I'm sure I was thinking, 'Oh, my God, this is it! This is it! We're going to get married!'

As I held my breath, he leaned in and gave me a gentle kiss on the lips. Then he moved down slowly past my crop top to my exposed midriff and kissed my belly button . . . And then he just walked away without saying another word! It was almost like he felt sorry for me and thought I needed something in return for all those weeks of devotion!

Nothing else happened with Peter, but I do think he's a nice bloke – I was so young and innocent, I'm sure he thought it was best to stay away. I probably wasn't cool enough for him at the time, either. In the past he'd gone out with Mel Blatt from All Saints, but I was just this sweet little girl in a rubbish pop group.

Some years later, when I joined Steps, I gave my number to someone to pass on to him, but he never called. Then, during a tour, when we were at the height of our fame, I was standing in baggage reclaim at Heathrow, having flown in from South Africa, and there was a voicemail from Peter on my mobile: 'Hi Claire, it's Pete. I just wanted to say hello,' he said. 'I know this message is about two years too late, but I hear you're doing really well now and just wondered if you wanted to get together?'

I couldn't believe it. I just kept saying, 'Oh, my God!' and making the rest of the band listen to it because they all knew how much I'd fancied him. But I decided not to call him back as I was seeing someone else by that point, and I wasn't interested in him any more.

I loved the year I spent in TSD and, every time I came off tour, I'd have a good two weeks of feeling really down in the dumps because I'd got so used to the adrenalin rush of performing and being on the road with the other acts. It was such fun and everyone was so nice – I never remember any diva-like behaviour. But the good times weren't to last long – our first single 'Heart & Soul' didn't do well, charting at sixty-nine, and our second single 'Baby I Love You' was also a flop and only made it to number sixty-four. It just wasn't working.

One day, in August 1996, Paul Fitzgerald called out of the blue and said, 'I just thought I'd let you know they're not going to renew your contract, so you have to decide what you want to do.' I was devastated. Paul didn't get in touch again and I didn't ring him back. His call was a brush-off really, so we found ourselves without management. We'd been an earner for him while we were signed, but we hadn't been successful.

Cossie and I decided to carry on by ourselves for a while, so Cossie called Bonnie to tell her. I'd never really got along with Bonnie – we were like chalk and cheese and there was no love lost between us. I felt that she was more interested in partying than taking the band seriously, so I wasn't sorry I wouldn't be seeing her any more. We found another girl called Suzie to join us and managed to get a couple of auditions. We went to Germany to meet with a record company, but when we got back to London, Cossie got a call from them to say they wanted her but not Suzie and me. Cossie was a bit older than I was and had already had a record deal before TSD, so this was a chance for her and, understandably, she felt she had to take it. We'd become best friends and I loved her to bits, so I was sad I wouldn't be working with her.

So that was the end of TSD. It seemed my singing career was over before it had even begun.

It was really difficult to be back at home with Mum and Dad after that year with TSD. Singing professionally was my dream come true and now it lay in tatters. I felt really down, but being young helped and I tried to focus on finding work. I needed to earn some money because what I'd earned with TSD had run out.

I probably could have gone back to the fabric shop, but I was too embarrassed, so I joined a temp agency and started doing reception work. For about three months I worked behind the desk at a hotel health spa, then I just temped wherever I was sent.

I was nineteen, still a virgin and professionally single. I suppose I've always been a bit of a romantic idealist and I wanted that love-at-first-sight, head-over-heels kind of feeling I'd experienced with Doug and Peter Andre. Looking back, I realize they were just huge crushes of the type most teenage girls have at some point. Guys asked me out, but I'd either see them once then never speak to them again, or I'd make some excuse as to why I couldn't go. I was just very bad at dating. I remember one time sitting in the airing cupboard in my parents' bedroom for hours, holding the phone and trying to pluck up the courage to dump someone. Mum and Dad still laugh at me now for doing that. But that's me all over – if I have to face something tricky, I'd rather just bury my head in the sand (or sit in the airing cupboard!).

After several months of temping and moping around feeling really sorry for myself, my mum had a word with me. 'Look, you're miserable, Claire,' she said. 'You know you miss singing, but if you want to make a career out of it, you're going to have to get out there and do it.'

It was what I needed to hear.

After her pep talk, Mum started getting *The Stage*, which is the newspaper for the performing arts industry, and we'd go through it together every week, circling auditions. Mum spotted the ad for Steps, which was looking for young, enthusiastic singers for a boy/girl group. So I stuck my demo tape in an envelope along with a photo and a flyer for TSD, circling my face on the flyer just to make sure they were in no doubt as to which one I was! I was temping for the Burger King head office in Uxbridge at the time and used the company's franking machine to send out all my tapes. Cheeky, I know!

May 1997 was a good month: I won Temp of the Month, which I was chuffed about, and I also got a call-back to audition for Steps. I'd sent out dozens of tapes, but Steps was the only one I got a reply from. They called to give me the details of the audition and I immediately started panicking. Auditions terrified me because I'd only ever done them at school and I just didn't have that stage-school confidence.

'I don't want to go. I don't think I should go,' I kept saying to Mum.

'You'll be fine,' she always said soothingly. 'I know you can do it.'

She managed to calm my nerves and, the night before, I rehearsed the tracks I was going to sing in our kitchen: Tina Turner's 'River Deep, Mountain High' and Eternal's 'I Am Blessed'.

The audition was at Bourne Hall in Ewell, Surrey and I drove there in my little Renault 5 with my sister Gemma, who I'd taken along for moral support. I was wearing a blue striped catsuit with wide legs, and trainers, and I had a black hoodie tied around my hips to hide my bum. Probably not the best look, but it was fashionable at the time.

When I had answered the ad in *The Stage* there was no mention of Steps being a line-dancing pop group but, when I arrived, they asked me to do a dance audition first. Rodeo Ruth had done the choreography – she was a big name in line dancing, which was a huge trend at the time. The routine we learnt was to '5, 6, 7, 8', which became Steps' first single.

The boys and girls were split into separate groups to do the routine and Rodeo Ruth was above us on the stage showing us the moves. Dancing isn't my strong point, but

I was there so I thought, 'Right, I might as well give it a go and if I just keep smiling, maybe they'll overlook the fact that I'm not doing it properly!' I'd had a bit of experience picking up dance routines from my time in TSD and I'd been to a couple of line-dancing classes with Melanie because she loved it.

Faye and Lee both stood out at the audition. As we scanned the hall of hopefuls, Gemma and I guessed both of them would make it through. Faye was just so beautiful – she had this gorgeous curly bobbed hair that was really blonde, and was wearing a pair of copper-coloured PVC trousers. You could tell by the way she carried herself that she had something going on. And Lee was the best-looking guy there.

When it was time for the singing audition we got taken one by one from the hall to a separate room with a video camera. In the room was Tim Byrne, who became our manager – he had blond hair and glasses, and seemed quite serious, although as I got to know him I found out he had a fun side. He had started out as a TV producer on *The Chart Show* and a kids' Saturday morning show called *Motormouth*. Early on, I clocked that he was fiercely ambitious and was definitely going places.

Also in the room were Steve Crosby and Barry Upton, who wrote '5, 6, 7, 8'. Steve was married to Rodeo Ruth and was quite short, with black hair and a goatee beard. He seemed really nice. Barry had been in one of the Brotherhood of Man line-ups and looked like the classic has-been pop star: he had a blond mullet hairdo and was wearing jeans and a white vest with really big arm holes. He accompanied me on his guitar while I sang 'River Deep, Mountain High', which he did OK. But when it came to Eternal's 'I Am Blessed', he said, 'Yeah, I think I know it,' then went on to play the wrong tune and completely messed me up! I was fuming at the time, but looking back it was quite funny. I found out later that Barry didn't want me in Steps – he wanted a girl who was Geri in a Spice Girls tribute band. She had massive boobs, but she couldn't sing a note!

After my singing audition there was a break in the schedule. When I came out of the room Faye walked over to me and said, 'Was that you singing in there? You've got a great voice.'

I think I was so bloody loud that everyone in the hall could hear me! If only I'd known back then the trouble my 'great' voice would go on to cause in Steps . . .

3

CLAIRE FROM STEPS

'We want you to be in the band, Claire,' said Tim. 'We think you've got a great voice and everything but, if you want to do it, you're going to have to lose weight.'

'Yeah, of course I'll lose weight. Definitely!' I replied enthusiastically.

The group of hopefuls had been whittled down after the singing audition so that there were about ten of us still in the running. Tim and Steve had taken everyone aside to speak to them individually.

I was ten stone at the time – not big at all, especially as I'm 5ft 6in – and I wore a size 10. My catsuit and hoodie probably didn't make the best of my figure, but there was no way I could be considered fat. I was so excited, though, all I could think about was finding a phone box to call Mum and tell her I'd been successful. It was the first time I was conscious that perhaps I was bigger than the other girls but I didn't dwell on it. I had no idea that Tim's comment about my weight would come to haunt me during my time in Steps.

Faye, Lee and I met H and Lisa briefly at the audition. They'd been in the original line-up of Steps with three other people and the band had already done loads of showcases. Simon Cowell was going to sign them at one point – he was big on novelty acts – but he ended up passing on it.

Lisa was wearing huge platform shoes and a tiny baby-doll dress and was brimming with confidence. She seemed very self-assured wasn't afraid to speak her mind. H was incredibly excitable and I liked him instantly – he was so bubbly and friendly. Because they were already in the band, the three of us felt a bit like they were pop stars already.

I thought Faye was sweet and friendly and seemed very calm, whereas Lee came across as quite serious – the strong, silent type. Both of them were good dancers and very fit.

After the audition, it was a couple of months before the band got together for rehearsals. The girls still had jobs to finish – Faye was singing in the Windows restaurant at the Hilton in Park Lane, and Lisa was working at Butlins. H had to move from Wales and Lee was finishing stage school.

I focused on my diet during that period and started doing some exercise, and it paid off. Melanie and I did a step class every Tuesday and I went back to the turkey and pea diet the choreographer for TSD had put us on. When I arrived to start rehearsals for '5, 6, 7, 8', Tim said, 'Oh, wow, Claire, you look great! You've lost loads of weight!'

'Really, do you think so?' I said, batting off the compliment, but inside I felt really proud that I'd pleased him.

I'd actually only lost seven pounds since I'd seen him at the audition, so I was nine and a half stone, but I suppose the exercise had toned me up and made a difference. I had a tan, too, as I'd been on holiday to the Dominican Republic with my family, and I was wearing tight cycling shorts.

When I started working with Steps I'd just turned twenty, was still living at home with Mum and Dad, and was STILL a virgin! I was sheltered and a bit naïve and I wanted to be liked by everyone. The rest of the band was older than me: Lee is three years older, the girls are both two-and-a-bit years older and H is just a year older. Obviously, now that we're all in our thirties the age difference means nothing, but back then it seemed vast.

Because I'd never been to stage school, I felt lucky I'd managed to break into the industry. Lisa had been to the Italia Conti Academy in London and Lee was at Laine Theatre Arts in Epsom. Faye had trained to be a dancer and H had always been involved in amateur dramatics outside school.

I got on really well with Faye initially – she became like a big sister to me and stayed at my house a few times. We used to stay up and chat about girly stuff or, if I went to bed early, she'd sit downstairs and natter with my mum for ages. Mum even did her washing once when we were really busy.

H also stayed over at mine a lot. We'd clicked with each other from day one, probably because we were close in age and liked the same music, and he was a bit of a homebody, just like me.

In fact, Lisa had trouble understanding me in the early days because she loved to go out and party and I didn't. I liked to be at home and she didn't really get that, plus we didn't have much in common – I'd say we were complete opposites.

At the beginning Lee and I clashed quite a lot – maybe some of it was down to the fact that I was the youngest and he was the eldest. But while I never banged on about TSD, there *were* certain things I knew about the business side of things, simply because I'd already been in a band with a record deal. So I knew, for example, that there were certain things you needed lawyers to look at, but I don't think Lee took me seriously when I made this point early on. I'm sure he thought I didn't know what I was talking about, but we never had massive rows – I didn't retaliate when he dismissed my ideas. Lee and I have always had a real love/hate relationship and we both still say that now. Sometimes we'd get on like a house on fire and sit in each other's rooms and watch movies together, but other times we'd really clash. But one thing that always frustrated me about being in Steps was that being the youngest – and maybe a bit too laidback – everyone assumed I was stupid and didn't listen to me half the time. I definitely felt like the baby of the band.

We rehearsed '5, 6, 7, 8' for two weeks to get ready to perform it in a showcase for Jive Records and Pete Waterman, in the hope they'd want to sign us up. Pete owned another label with Jive called EBUL and I knew that he was an incredibly successful music producer who'd launched the singing careers of Kylie, Rick Astley and Jason Donovan, so I was pretty nervous about meeting him.

Rodeo Ruth had taught us the routine, and we just kept going over and over it again so that by the end of that fortnight we were so tight. On the day of the showcase we'd coordinated our outfits – we all wore black and white – and we were completely together on everything. Pete wasn't intimidating at all – just really friendly and positive. After the performance, we sat down and they asked us loads of questions, then we got signed – just like that! In fact, we were signed as a seven-piece with Barry Upton and Steve Crosby. I think that to Lee, H, Lisa, Faye and myself that didn't seem right but we accepted it.

All we got for at least the first year of Steps was £50 a week 'per diems' (an allowance for daily expenses) when we were working – which was pretty much all the time. Thankfully, there was always a radio or TV plugger (someone whose job was to get us played on air or get us spots on television) around to buy us food and I was lucky because I lived at home with Mum and Dad, so my per diems were spent on clothes. But Lisa, Lee and H were sharing a flat, and I don't know how they managed.

*

Soon after we got signed, we went to Marbella in Spain to shoot the video for '5, 6, 7, 8'. Because the shoot was on the beach, they wanted the girls to wear bikinis. I panicked straightaway. There was no way I wanted to expose my hips and bum in bikini bottoms, so I asked for a bikini that had one of those matching miniskirts. I think the poor stylist had to hunt high and low to find one, but eventually she did and I ended up wearing an orange bikini with matching mini for the video.

The thing is, I would never have worn a bikini on holiday without tying a sarong around my waist. I never minded my top half being exposed because of my tiny waist, small boobs and a flat stomach, but I thought my bum and legs were massive. These days I can appreciate the curve of my hips, which looks good in pencil skirts and figure-hugging dresses, but if you look at old Steps footage you'll never see me wearing anything that draws attention to my bum – I'm always wearing a crop top or a bikini top with hipsters.

I'd already made a couple of videos with TSD, but they were both shot in a studio and we never got to go abroad, so making the video for '5, 6, 7, 8' was fun – and we didn't just fly in and fly out again; we had a couple of days there. I remember us all lying on sunbeds and the director coming around and poking us to make sure we weren't burning before shooting the video!

It was a good trip and we were all excited – none of us knew what was going to happen at that point or had any idea of the successes Steps would go on to achieve. We didn't know how well the first single would do or what would come after it; we were all just young, happy and enjoying being part of something.

On that trip H told me he was gay. We were heading out one evening and, as we were walking upstairs into a club in Puerto Banus, he said, 'Claire, I need to speak to you later. I really need to tell you something.'

All night I kept thinking, 'Oh, God! He's going to tell me he fancies me.' I swear I was convinced he wanted to go out with me and I was going to have to tell him I didn't like him in that way.

When we got back to our hotel that night we were drunk, but we ordered another four beers and a big bag of Wotsits and took them down to the beach. We found a spot to sit among the stacked-up sunbeds and he just came right out with it and told me he was gay. I was hugely relieved!

'Is that all?' I replied. 'That's fine. Thank God for that!'

When I told the others later, they couldn't believe I hadn't twigged and were all saying, 'Are you having a laugh? Did you *really* not know that?'

H didn't strike me as being camp, I suppose – I thought he was just young and a bit overenthusiastic!

Before that trip to Spain I'd never really had a lot of alcohol. I'd got very drunk when I was seventeen with Hayley Pile and Melanie and it had really put me off drinking. We were at Mel's mate Lorraine's house having a party because her parents were away and I drank a whole bottle of sweet wine and threw up everywhere. I was in the toilet being sick and Hayley was trying to force a packet of crisps on me, saying, 'Have these, Claire, they'll make you feel better.' Eventually, she put me to bed with a bucket and manoeuvred me into the recovery position so I wouldn't choke on my own vomit. The next day I felt so ill I went straight to bed when I got home, after sheepishly telling my parents I was exhausted after staying up all night. After that I'd just have a little bit to drink – usually one brandy and Coke.

When the video shoot was over we had a wrap party in the director's room, and I spied a bottle of Jack Daniels. For some reason I thought, 'Right, I'll drink that!' It was only a small bottle, but I drank the whole lot. It was the first time I'd been drunk with the band and I ended up falling asleep on the bathroom floor after throwing up.

Eventually, I woke up and put myself to bed, but the next day we had to fly home and I woke up fifteen minutes before we had to leave. I hadn't packed anything and, because I was the only one still living at home, I was the only one with a family-size suitcase so I had everyone's costumes to put in!

I frantically chucked everything into the suitcase, then all the way to the airport I sat by the window of the coach with my cheap sunglasses on, with my head pounding, thinking, 'Oh, my God. I'm going to be sick, I'm going to be sick!'

As soon as we got to the airport at Malaga I had to have a Burger King – my excuse was that it was the only way to get rid of my hangover. It didn't work and I still felt like shit, only now I was both hungover *and* feeling guilty because no one else had resorted to junk food. It was only 10 a.m. and I'd stuffed down a burger and fries; I felt terrible the whole way home.

But the nightmare wasn't over just yet. Sitting on the plane, I was suddenly aware that my name was being called out over the tannoy and, honestly, my first thought was, 'They're going to throw me off the plane because I'm drunk.' But because my dad works in the air-freight business, he knew someone that worked for the airline we were travelling with and he had actually arranged for us to have a bottle of champagne on the plane to say congratulations for our first video. The stewardess asked if I'd like her to open it but I just said, 'No, thanks, I'll take it home with me,' while trying my hardest not to retch at the thought of more alcohol.

That was my first taste of celebrity excess – as tame as it was! I'd only just turned twenty the month before and didn't know how to handle my liquor.

When we got back to London we started playing gigs all over the country for six weeks on the run up to '5, 6, 7, 8' being released, to try to generate a groundswell of support. We played loads of under-18s gigs at nightclubs, as well as places like sports centres.

The first time we went on one of those tours, it was arranged that we would all meet up first with the tour manager, Barry James, outside the London Weekend Television studios on the Southbank in London. Barry was a big black guy with plaited hair and not at all who you'd expect to be looking after Steps: I'm sure he'd rather have been with a really cool urban R&B band, but instead he was landed with us!

We climbed into a Toyota Previa people carrier – which was to become like a best friend as we spent so much time in it, all ridiculously excited to be sitting in the back of the Prev. As we pulled away, Janet Jackson's 'Together Again' was playing on the radio and we all started singing along – it kind of became our anthem after that. Of course, about an hour up the M1 we were already bored!

We started to get to know each other much better on those trips to gigs up north because we spent so much time cooped up together in the Prev and sharing rooms in B&Bs. We used to have three beds in the girls' room so Faye, Lisa and I could all be together.

We really worked our asses off, which is one of the reasons why this whole *X Factor* thing kind of annoys me. Those contestants think they work hard, but they really don't. To be on a TV show for ten weeks, then instantly become one of the most famous people in the country – that's the easy way! We, on the other hand, were sometimes doing three gigs a night in different clubs. We'd kick things off at an under-18s gig, then we'd be in nightclubs that just played dance music until 5 a.m. And it was always the same routine, of course: we'd start with our backs to the audience, then we'd all get into position on a different count. Every single time that fiddle started at the beginning of '5, 6, 7, 8' you could see our shoulders hunch as we got into position. We did the same thing for weeks on end, and the gigs all started to blur into one.

Another Level was starting out at the same time as us and we'd often go to clubs after they'd been there and see all their postcards and flyers lying around. We kind of followed them around the country.

Nothing about the touring was glamorous. We got dressed in a lot of offices and back rooms; one night we performed on the poorest excuse for a stage I've ever seen – it was literally a block of wood that was just big enough for us to squeeze on to. God only knows how we managed to do a routine on it. Often we'd just perform in the middle of the dance floor and all the clubbers would stand around and watch, but I don't ever remember being booed or jeered.

Sometimes Faye and Lisa hung out at the clubs afterwards, but most of the time we went back to our B&B or drove back to London if we didn't have any gigs the next day. The hours were long and it was tiring, and because we all lived in different areas, someone would have to get dropped off last. And because I lived on the outskirts of London, near the two major motorways we usually took, the M4 and the M40, it seemed to be me who was most often picked up last or dropped off first. To make it fair, the others decided that even if we were on the M4 or the M40, the route should be changed so that someone else could be dropped off first and I'd have to stay in the van out of principle as we drove into central London and out again! I'd be so close to home one minute, then so far! Later when we were flying abroad to do gigs, there were even times when I was picked up first, even though I lived 10 minutes down the road from Heathrow, and we'd then have to travel miles in the wrong direction to south London to pick up the others.

That was the first little thing where I felt the others were having a dig at me. Looking back, I realize I shouldn't have taken it personally, but at the time I did. I probably got a bit moody about it and sulked because that's what I used to do. I know I wouldn't put up with it now – I'd get myself to where we had to be.

Just before '5, 6, 7, 8' was released we did another show-case at the Atlantic Bar & Grill in Piccadilly, London. There, Pete Waterman introduced us to the industry and the media as 'Abba on speed'. We performed '5, 6, 7, 8' and another song that never became a single.

It was at that event that we were introduced to Reece Hill, who was head of promotions at the record label and who became our TV plugger. Of course I noticed that he was tall, dark and handsome, with lovely brown eyes! He seemed nice, too, but I didn't think more of it than that. I was a bit overwhelmed by the whole event, to be honest. I was never good in a room full of people I didn't know; I'd just stand back and let everyone else do the talking. I'm better at it now, because with Steps I was put into situations where I had no choice but to talk to people, but it's not a natural thing for me. I'm always far too worried about what people will think of me. Luckily, it was hard to get a word in edgeways with the rest of the band, anyway! None of them was shy and they were happy to do the talking – and I was happy to let them.

'5, 6, 7, 8' was released in November 1997. H was convinced straightaway that it was going to be a number one and that the band was set to be massive. As it was, it entered at eighteen, but never got higher than fourteen, even though we sold around 290,000 copies of it. It ended up staying in the Top 40 for three months and was the biggest song of the 1990s not to reach the Top 10. That kind of thing happened to us a lot – there always seemed to be another single stopping us from getting a better chart position. In the case of '5, 6, 7, 8' it was Vanilla's 'No Way No Way'.

Every time we did a TV show the single nudged up the charts a bit, though. The first one was *5-LIVE* on Channel 5, not long after the station was launched, then we did lots of little ones: *Blue Peter*, and other kids' shows on Nickelodeon and the Disney Channel. Every now and then we'd get a bigger show: we did ITV's *Talking Telephone Numbers* with Phillip Schofield, and Charlotte Church was performing, too. She was just a kid at the time and I remember saying, 'Yeah, she's good but she'll never make it.' I must learn to keep my mouth shut!

We also managed to get on to the *Smash Hits* Poll Winners Party on BBC1 because our manager Tim produced it. Ant and Dec were presenting it and we were the reserve act. We did the warm-up in front of the audience, but we weren't actually meant to be on the telly. But Tim kept saying to everyone who won an award, 'We're running behind time, so you have to just go on and get your award and get off again.' Basically, he was trying to claw back two and a half minutes so we could run on and do our performance – and he pulled it off!

We were due to go on after Celine Dion, so she was standing backstage with us waiting. I was completely starstruck – she was someone who'd inspired me as a singer and I'd performed her songs at the Heath Tavern's karaoke competitions. All I could do was stare at her in awe, thinking how amazing she was. I was far too overwhelmed to say anything and I'm glad I didn't because I'm sure I would have embarrassed myself. She did turn round and say, 'I like your hair' to Faye, though, who still had a gorgeous curly blonde bob at the time. I was so jealous!

Of course, it was all about making it on to *Top Of The Pops*. We didn't manage it at first – the single went up and down for ages, but when it made it to fourteen in the chart, we got to perform on the show.

I can't explain the excitement of performing on that first show. I used to watch *Top Of The Pops* religiously as a kid and absolutely loved it. It used to be on every Thursday evening at seven o'clock on BBC1, right before *EastEnders*. As soon as I heard the music start I'd settle down in front of the telly and wait for the chart countdown. It was a huge part of growing up for all of us, I think. I'd always dreamt of being on *Top Of The Pops* but I had never expected it to become reality, especially after I'd been in TSD and that hadn't worked out. I can't imagine there are many people who have that kind of dream and the faith that it'll actually come true.

To be honest, I don't think I ever really thought Steps would be as successful as it was – who could have predicted that a line-dancing pop group with a choreographed routine for every song would capture the public imagination the way it did?

All I remember from that first show is that Vanilla was on the bill with us; I was so happy and excited it all became a bit of a blur. It was a big deal to get on to *TOTP* and, in the grand scheme of things, it hadn't taken us that long to do it – even though it had felt like it when we were slogging our guts out doing those gigs to promote the single. They paid off in the end!

The record company had bought us new outfits for the performance from Hyper Hyper in Kensington, which was a big store that housed loads of designer concessions. It was such a relief, because we'd literally worn the same outfit for months on end – mine was red PVC trousers and a red mesh, long-sleeved top with a bra underneath. It stank, even though it was always getting washed! For *TOTP* I wore a brown leopard-print corset and brown trousers.

Reece was responsible for getting us on to *TOTP*. After we'd started doing TV shows he was always around and he used to travel in the Prev with us. Nine years older than me, he was so charming and was always making us laugh. He's the king of the crap joke, and very quick-witted. That's when I began to really fancy him – in fact, I'm sure we all had a little crush on him at the beginning.

Nothing happened, though, until December 1997 when Jive had a Christmas party in the Aldwych disused tube station. All of us had had quite a bit to drink and I think a few people must have told Reece that I fancied him; although we were all grown-ups, it felt like being back at school again – it was all very, 'My mate fancies you.'

We were all standing in this huge old lift but, gradually, the others began to leave one by one on purpose so Reece and I could be alone. And that's when we had our first kiss. I knew Reece had a girlfriend and that he lived with her, too, so at that point I wasn't expecting anything to come of it. But I didn't regret the kiss – it had felt lovely.

When I went home for Christmas, Doug was visiting from America and I had a snog with him, too. And at another party I kissed an American guy called Trey Parker, who'd been in a band called E.Y.C. He'd been one of my many crushes when I was younger. So, in terms of snogs, I had a very good Christmas that year!

I didn't see Reece for about six weeks after our kiss. When the holidays were over, Steps went into the studio to record, so there were no TV shows lined up and therefore no reason to bump into each other.

Our second single was to be a cover of a Bananarama song called 'Last Thing On My Mind'. The song is very Abba-esque, and we got to go to Cuba to shoot the video! Originally, the idea was for all our singles to involve line dancing, but when we got into Jive and PWL, I think they spotted something different in us. They saw the chemistry we had as a band and the way people took to us, and felt we were more than just a line-dancing novelty act. After that Barry Upton and Steve Crosby were no longer our writers and weren't involved in the band but Tim Byrne continued to manage us, alongside Victoria Blood, who had previously worked for record label BMG.

On the run-up to the release of the single, in February 1998, I started spending a bit more time with Reece because we were doing lots of TV shows. I think we both knew we liked each other, but he was still in a proper long-term relationship so nothing was said.

I'd bought myself a pager after Christmas because I couldn't afford a mobile phone and Reece was really the only person who ever paged me. I found myself staring at it all the time, thinking, 'Oh, why aren't you paging me?!' But I never went out of my way to make anything happen, because of his girlfriend.

Then Reece got us on to *Top Of The Pops* to perform 'Last Thing On My Mind' – the single had stormed into the Top 10 after its release in April, peaking at number six. It was the start of us becoming *TOTP* regulars.

After the show, he came over to me before we got into the Prev to go home. 'Do you fancy going out one night?' he asked, smiling.

My stomach was flipping over because I was so excited, but I tried to act cool. 'Er, yeah, OK then, what did you have in mind?' I replied, looking as nonchalant as I could.

'How about dinner and a movie?'

'My perfect night out,' I said. 'It's a date.'

He took me to a cinema in High Wycombe for our date and, although I don't remember what we saw, I remember what we ate! There was a Mongolian barbecue at the Holiday Inn next door, so we decided to have that before going to see the film. I had butterflies all night because I was so excited to be with him. I'd never felt so relaxed with a guy before. I liked him A LOT.

After that we were kind of dating I suppose, and it was easy for us to see a lot of each other because we were working together so much. We often had to go on little trips up north because the band had been booked to do TV shows and we'd stay the night in hotels. We never slept together during that time, but we'd have a snog and mess around.

Back in London, Reece and I went on a few dates, but most of the time we just ended up kissing in the car outside my parents' house. It was like being a teenager all over again! But there was no getting away from it: Reece, who was thirty at the time, was still living with his girlfriend, Bonnie. They'd been going out together since they were teenagers, but he'd told me things weren't good between them: they rowed a lot and had split up several times over the years. I secretly hoped he'd leave her for me, like any mistress would – it was still very early on in our relationship and it was easier to believe that. But, the fact was, he'd built a life with Bonnie.

I was very young, though, and all that mattered to me was that I loved him. I thought I'd been in love with Doug and Peter Andre, but I realized later that Pete was just a huge crush and Doug, I guess, was my teenage sweetheart.

Reece was the first guy I'd been on a grown-up date with who I really fancied and who I also thought of as a friend – the situation with his girlfriend had meant we had had to become friends first and we quickly realized we could talk to each other about anything. He always made me laugh, but he made me feel special, too, and I'd never had all of those things with a guy before.

I remember thinking, 'If I'm not going to be with this man, I'll never find anyone this perfect again.'

4

SUCCESS IS BITTERSWEET

'Claire, I've got something important to tell you,' said Reece, taking my hand. 'Bonnie's pregnant.'

His words took my breath away. It was a bombshell that shook me to my core and I burst into floods of tears. I hadn't seen it coming at all.

We were up in Newcastle to promote 'Last Thing on My Mind' and Reece had come into my hotel room to give me his news. As I sat next to him on the bed, crying, unable to find any words to express how devastated I was, Reece went on to explain that he and Bonnie had started trying for a baby before we'd got together, in an effort to save their relationship.

'It means we're going to have to stop seeing each other,' he said gently.

'I know,' I replied, sobbing into his shoulder.

'It's not what I want because I love you,' he whispered.

It was April, so we'd only been seeing each other for a

couple of months. We still hadn't slept together, but I'd fallen in love with him too. I knew nothing I could say would change things, so I just curled up into a little ball on the bed and stayed there for hours while Reece held me in his arms. I didn't know how I was going to cope with seeing him at work, knowing we couldn't be together. It was heart-breaking, but I knew there was no other option.

When we got back to London we tried our best to avoid each other, but it was impossible. We were doing lots of TV shows and Reece was always around the band, so it wasn't long before we found ourselves in situations where we were alone together – backstage at a TV studio or in a hotel – and, within weeks, we'd slipped back into seeing each other again. When you're so strongly attracted to someone, it's very hard to keep your distance and I wanted to be with him all the time. I knew he wasn't just another crush.

We carried on our affair through the rest of Bonnie's pregnancy: I was only twenty and probably too young and selfish to appreciate the impact this could have had on her. I didn't know Bonnie – I'd never met her – so it didn't touch me in the same way it did Reece.

It was a couple of months before we slept together, but in June my parents went on holiday and, one night after we'd been out for dinner, Reece drove me home and I invited him to stay. That was the night I lost my virginity – in my single bed, at home. I always remember friends telling me about their first time and how awful it was or how much it hurt, but it wasn't like that for me at all. It was amazing! I think it was so good because I'd waited a long time and I was doing it with the person I was in love with. It just felt right.

We ended up doing it quite a few times that night! We thought we were being really quiet, but my sister's room was right below mine and she came stomping up the stairs, shouting, 'Will you two shut up!' and 'Don't pretend you're not doing anything!'

I'd never been in a rush to have sex – maybe part of that was down to feeling self-conscious about my body. Sleeping with someone is, ultimately, a very vulnerable position to put yourself in, and I've never felt free enough to just meet a guy at a party and go and have sex with him. Reece always made me feel good about my body, though. Right from the start, he used to say how much he loved my bum – and it wasn't because I made a point of saying how much I hated it. He never complimented me on my flat tummy or my boobs – it was always my bottom, the very part of my body I'd spent years trying to hide. I've even got notes from him that he wrote years ago, and they all start off with, 'I love your bum!'

That summer we released our third single 'One For Sorrow', and that's when things really began to take off for Steps in a big way. It achieved a chart position of number two – our highest ever – and sold a stonking 363,000 copies. But it was bittersweet for me.

Before it was released, Pete Waterman sat us all down in the studio and played our debut album *Step One* from start to finish. Then he played 'One For Sorrow' and told us it was going to be the next single from the album. I was really chuffed because I was singing the whole track.

As the song faded, H came over and gave me a big hug, and said, 'Well done, Claire!' I only had a moment to feel pleased before the others started asking 'Why is she singing all of it?' and 'Why are you releasing a single where it's just Claire singing?'

It was almost as if I wasn't in the room! I can see now that of course we were all driven by a desire to be a success and to be in the spotlight – as is everyone who joins a band like ours – and I probably would have felt the same as them if I thought I was being overlooked. But at that time, whether they meant it that way or not, I felt as if the comments were a personal attack on me and it totally spoiled that feeling of being really proud that something I'd done had been chosen. Pete obviously thought it had turned out good enough to be the next single, but instead of feeling ecstatic, I felt really uncomfortable because of the way the others were reacting. It wasn't my fault it had been picked, but it was quite clear they were furious about it.

They got up and left the room without saying another word. From then on, it felt like those kind of petty rivalries started to rise to the surface more and more.

I was also made to feel awkward in September 1998 when we had an album launch for *Step One* ahead of 'Heartbeat' / 'Tragedy' being released in November. We'd already learnt the dance routine for 'Heartbeat' and we were performing it at the launch party at Sound Republic in Leicester Square.

At the sound check, however, a couple of the others suddenly piped up, 'We don't think Claire should be in the middle for this routine because a few of our friends and family have commented that she looks like the lead singer, and we don't like it. There is no lead singer.' As a result, I got shoved on the end for that song, and that's where I was from that day on whenever we performed the single.

After that, a huge deal was made of rotating us in and out of the middle because, for some reason, if you were in the middle, everyone assumed you were the lead singer. It actually became embarrassing when we were doing TV shows because we would all go through the camera scripts, to make sure we got shots on our bits. Now it seems quite petty but back then we all felt it was crucial we got our fair share of time in front of the camera.

Things were starting to get complicated in my personal life, too. Reece didn't want to be with Bonnie any more but I don't think he knew how not to be with her because they'd been together so long and, now that she was pregnant, it was even more difficult. Since we'd slept together, we'd tried to grab as much time as we could on our own, but we didn't really have anywhere to go and we had to be careful we weren't spotted. I was still living at home with my parents and, although they disapproved of the situation, they liked

Reece and allowed him to stay over as long as he slept in another bedroom, but he used to sneak in and out of my room before everyone else woke up.

Because we couldn't see each other as much as we wanted to, when we did get together we'd have sex anywhere and everywhere. We were at it like you wouldn't believe and, when I look back now, you'd never think we were the same couple! We did it on a train once on our way to a TV show in Manchester, in dressing rooms at gigs and TV shows, including *Top Of The Pops*, and in the car park of Hillingdon tube station – anywhere we could. And we'd stay up all night long, trying to make the most of the time we had together.

Reece had a tiny MG sports car at the time and we even managed to do it in that – afterwards I was covered in bruises from head to toe! We used to park the car in the next road to where my mum and dad lived, just in front of a hedge so there was no house overlooking us. But there *was* a house right behind us with a big security light that would be on the whole time! I'll never know how we didn't get busted.

Because we got to see each other a lot through work, we were able to sneak in little snogs and some hand-holding. And Reece would volunteer to drive me home because my house was on the way to his place in Richmond: he was always saying to the record company, 'Oh, I'm going past Claire's house,' so he could deliver things to me and we'd be able to see each other.

The band knew about our affair – it would have been impossible to hide it from them because Reece worked so closely with us. It was very stressful, though, and I worried constantly about whether we were going to be seen or if the papers would find out about it. We were always trying to think up places to go where no one would know us so we could walk down the street without the risk of being recognized. I was totally in love with Reece, but the situation meant I felt anxious a lot of the time.

Sadly, there were lots of occasions, too, when I desperately wanted to see Reece and I couldn't because he had to be with Bonnie. Just before my twenty-first birthday we'd gone to Spain with the band to do a TV show. Reece took me down to the beach and gave me a Tiffany necklace and key ring – they were beautiful, and the first expensive presents anyone had ever bought me. But he couldn't be at my party, which was what I wanted more than anything. He was never there to share those special moments.

After we released 'Heartbeat'/'Tragedy' in November, our management also told us we'd be doing a nationwide theatre tour the following March. None of us in the band could believe it and we were all saying, 'Are you sure people will buy tickets?' But it was a sell-out and, even before we did the tour, there were already plans to put on a thirty-five-date arena show before the end of 1999.

This should have been the start of the most exciting and fun time of my life, but it was actually the beginning of things being awful for me for a very long time. From then on, my weight started to drop because of the stress of my relationship with Reece, our punishing work schedule, and the tensions in the band that had begun to surface, too.

Christmas 1998 was a very tough time. Reece's daughter, Olivia, was born on 30 December. He came over to my house that day, clutching a photograph of him holding her. We didn't sleep together – Reece sat on the bench in our kitchen and I sat on the floor in front of him with my head resting on his leg. We didn't say much; we just wanted to be together. He was obviously ecstatic that he'd just had a daughter, but I felt like someone had stabbed me in the heart. I wanted to be with Reece so much, but I was on my own through most of the holidays because of course he had to be with Bonnie and Olivia.

I wouldn't wish being 'the mistress' on my worst enemy, but I don't expect anyone to feel sorry for me. I knew Reece was in a relationship when I started seeing him, but I was very young and I just loved him so much that I couldn't imagine how I could be without him. And I didn't want to be without him because I'd never felt that way about any man.

I convinced myself that I was fine with the fact that he'd had a baby, but in reality it felt constantly as though I'd had the wind sucked out of me. It was the worst feeling in the world.

Even the news we'd got our first number one with 'Heartbeat'/'Tragedy' on 2 January 1999 could only cheer me up for a few hours. It had been hanging around the Top 10 for weeks but, over Christmas, our up-tempo version of the

Bee Gees' 'Tragedy', with its easy dance moves, hit the spot and it ended up staying in the Top 40 for sixteen weeks, selling more than a million copies. It was a massive hit.

So while my career was soaring with our first number-one single, my personal life was a complete and utter mess. I was all over the place, and Reece and I decided not to see each other for a couple of weeks. He wanted to enjoy his baby – you don't get those moments very often, so it was understandable. I needed space, too – partly because I was feeling guilty about our affair, but also because as the weeks passed I was still finding it hard to accept that the man I loved had a baby with someone else: I was devastated that we would never share the experience of having our first child together. All of a sudden there was this little person who wasn't mine and I really wanted it to be *us* sharing that experience. Because I was so young I couldn't really see beyond that way of thinking, and it bothered me for a long time afterwards.

At this point I was already thin. I'd become conscious of my weight after being told at the audition I was effectively too big to be in the band, but during 1999 my weight plummeted to just under eight stone – the thinnest I'd ever been. It was partly down to the stress of my relationship with Reece and worrying about whether I'd get to see him or whether we'd have to split up. For a while, I just didn't feel hungry and stopped thinking about eating.

I was still living with my parents and they weren't happy

with the situation – they put up with a lot at this point, and it put a lot of strain on them. They still allowed Reece to come over, but I'm sure that if, in the future, my daughter brought a man home who was practically married and had a baby, then I wouldn't want him in the house, either. I'd forbid her to see him!

During the times I was away with the band, Reece would still go round to see Mum and Dad. Apparently, they'd confront him over it, and say, 'What's going on? What are you going to do? Are you going to split up with Bonnie?' Basically, they told him he couldn't carry on the way he was. It was hard for Reece, too, because he never wanted to leave Olivia. He might have fallen out of love with Bonnie, but he loved his little girl to bits and he's a fantastic dad.

After the success of 'Tragedy', the band's workload seemed to triple – we were so busy and hardly ever had a day off. We were regularly working sixteen-hour days and it took its toll on all of us I think – we were all exhausted.

In March, our fifth single 'Better Best Forgotten' was released – it went straight in at number two, but was kept off the top spot by Boyzone's Comic Relief single 'When The Going Gets Tough'. In the same month, we performed a medley of Abba hits at the Brit Awards alongside other acts, including Billie and B*Witched.

The theatre tour kicked off in Bristol on 6 March and we were on the road for about six weeks. Every day I'd get myself a Happy Meal from McDonald's around lunchtime before I went to the venue – a cheeseburger, small fries and a Coke. It was hardly a balanced diet and it was all I'd have to eat all day, even though I had demanding dance routines to perform every night.

One day, our tour manager, John Procter, started asking the catering staff whether I was coming in for a meal or not. He'd noticed I wasn't eating and started checking every day to find out what I'd had, so I began eating my catered meal every day – usually chicken and vegetables. At least it was healthier than a burger and chips, but it was still all I'd eat for the entire day.

When I watch footage of Steps from that time, particularly the video for 'Better Best Forgotten', I look horribly thin. If I'd have *really* seen myself back then I'd have thought, 'You're ill, there's something wrong with you.'

By now, my weight loss wasn't due to stress taking my appetite away. I actually thought I was fat and was seriously limiting what I ate. I couldn't see that in reality I was a bag of bones: I was drowning in my size 8 clothes but I was still pinching fictitious bits of fat and obsessing over them. When I look back at pictures of me on that tour, there isn't a spare inch of flesh anywhere on my body, but still I focused on being as thin as possible.

I remember one night being backstage for our quick costume change. I was standing there with a pair of hipsters that barely stayed up, grabbing my thighs and saying to my friend Shelina, who was one of our backing dancers, 'I still need to get rid of this little bit.' There was nothing there, but I had a totally distorted view of my body; anyone else would have looked at me and assumed I was sick as there wasn't an ounce of fat on me.

I used to convince myself I wasn't hungry and that I didn't need to eat, but I was tired all the time and from the beginning of the year I'd been picking up colds and suffering badly with tonsillitis. When we sang at the Brits I was so ill with tonsillitis I missed rehearsals and was in bed right up until we had to perform, and I rushed away before the after-party. I was totally exhausted. I suppose I just wasn't feeding my body properly – it wasn't getting the right nutrition.

I didn't realize I had a problem at that time, but now I can understand that I was controlling what I ate because it seemed the only choice I had in life. My relationship with Reece was out of my control as it wasn't up to me when I saw him because he had a girlfriend and a baby at home – I couldn't even call him in case he was with Bonnie. I wasn't in control of what happened with the band, and I didn't even live in my own house, which meant I still had to observe my parents' rules to a certain extent. Sometimes I'd come home in the small hours of the morning if I'd been out at an event or with Reece, and my mum would be still up waiting for me!

When the theatre tour was over in April, things hit an all-time low.

Reece was obviously having a bad time at home. Any man who has an affair is going to say, 'My home life is awful', but the things that weren't great between him and Bonnie before I came on to the scene had just got worse. He stayed for Olivia's sake, but anyone with kids knows that having a child to save a relationship can never work. If it's already on the rocks, adding a new baby into the mix is going to kill the relationship stone dead. Babies are stressful, especially during those first few months and if your relationship isn't solid, you'll never get through it.

At that point I don't think Bonnie knew Reece was having an affair, but she must have known something was wrong because he wasn't showing any interest in her: he was never home as he was either at work, or with me.

Olivia was about four months old when Reece called me out of the blue one day and said we had to end it. Things were difficult at home with the baby and he needed to be there for Bonnie. The only thing he thought he could do to make the situation better was to end our relationship.

It was just before I was due to go into hospital to have my tonsils out. By now, the bouts of tonsillitis had gone on for months and I felt terrible as a result. I had gone to see a specialist about my throat and he had recommended that I should have my tonsils taken out as soon as possible because I couldn't afford to keep getting ill. I was terrified about it, though, and I kept thinking, 'What if the surgeons damage my throat? If I lose my voice or it sounds different, what'll I do then?'

I was more miserable than I'd ever been in my life and was missing Reece dreadfully. He'd changed his mobile number and didn't contact me at all when I was in hospital, or when I was recovering at home afterwards.

I began to get even skinnier. On top of the fact I was hardly eating anything before the operation, after I'd had the op, I totally lost my appetite: I was in so much pain anything I tried to eat hurt like hell. The morning after I'd had my tonsils taken out I was offered toast and cornflakes for breakfast, and I thought, 'There's no way I'm eating that!' so I asked for ice cream instead. Even that caused pain from my ears right down my throat. I think I managed a bit of soup and that was about it, and for at least three weeks afterwards I ate hardly anything at all.

The result was that I lost more weight and, inevitably, my periods stopped. I actually believed I might be pregnant at one point and remember thinking, 'Shit! What am I going to do?' but I didn't tell anyone. My mind kept going round in circles, worrying about how I could bring a baby into the world when my personal life was such a mess.

To this day I don't know if I was pregnant and had an early miscarriage, but my periods eventually returned a few weeks later. I think it was probably just down to my body being so starved of nutrition and the fact that I felt incredibly stressed and unhappy. But for a long time afterwards my periods were erratic, and I could go a couple of months without having one.

I don't remember anyone in the band commenting on my weight loss, but during that time I was so unhappy and tired all the time, it must have been obvious I didn't want to be there. I stopped putting any effort into learning new dance routines – in fact, they nicknamed me Lethargic Steps at one point – and wasn't interested in anything to do with the band.

Things got so bad that our management sat me down one day and asked what was wrong, but I covered up the fact I wasn't eating and just said I was tired. They sent me to see a doctor and I lied to him too about my diet, but he still did loads of blood tests and said my testosterone levels were very low. He gave me a shot of testosterone for energy, but I worried for ages afterwards that I was going to start growing a beard!

Going to see the doctor got the record company off my back for a while – in fact, no one ever mentioned my health again. The rest of the band knew what was going on with Reece and me, but naturally they were all preoccupied with their own lives.

When Reece had called me to end things it had been a very definite 'That's it' but, about four weeks later, he texted me and we started talking again. It wasn't long before we started seeing each other, too – as hard as we'd tried, we couldn't seem to stay apart. The fact was that we'd both been utterly miserable without each other.

Our joy was to be short-lived, though, because in June Bonnie found out about our affair.

I was in bed asleep one Sunday morning when my phone rang. The call was from a withheld number, which I didn't usually answer, but sometimes Reece would call me from a phone box, so I decided to pick it up. I heard a woman's voice I didn't recognize, then my blood ran cold when she told me she was Bonnie. She'd caught me off-guard as I'd just woken up, and felt disorientated.

I think she'd found Reece's phone bills with my number on them. We thought we'd been doing a really good job of keeping the affair secret, but obviously it wasn't good enough.

At first Bonnie kind of tricked me into believing that she was OK with everything. She kept saying, 'It's OK, I understand,' but then she just went ballistic. She kept on at me, trying to get the truth, and I denied it for a while until she told me that Reece had confessed. He hadn't, of course – she was calling my bluff in the hope I'd admit to it and she'd have confirmation of the affair.

While I was panicking that she'd found out, at the same time a part of me was glad she knew, because it meant Reece could finally leave her to be with me.

I was on the phone to Bonnie for quite a while; then I spoke to Reece, who told me her dad had had him up against a wall, threatening to batter him for what he'd done to her. It really was absolutely awful. Reece was pretty shaken up and I tried my best to reassure him that things would be OK. Ultimately, I think he was relieved she finally found out the truth and that he wouldn't have to be the one who told her.

Reece left Bonnie after that and went to stay with his sister, Tara: I think if he hadn't, Bonnie would have kicked him out. Olivia was only about six months old and I know it broke his heart to leave her behind. He had always said he wanted to leave Bonnie but that he couldn't face the thought of being without his daughter. It was terrible for him.

Almost as soon as Reece left home, Steps had to go to America to support Britney Spears on her 'Baby One More Time' tour. She was on the same record label as us and the story was that she'd remembered us from a show we'd done in Singapore a couple of years before, and asked if we could support her. I'm sure that was just a bit of record industry hype!

As usual, the timing couldn't have been worse. Before I left the UK, things were very difficult between Reece and Bonnie as they tried to work out issues relating to Olivia. It was clear to me that Bonnie didn't want me to be with Reece when he was looking after his daughter. Then she told her story to a tabloid newspaper and there were legal letters exchanged as we tried to stop it being published – it didn't work. It was all very unpleasant.

When the story came out, I was in the recording studio with the rest of the band and Pete Waterman. I was so upset, but Pete and his PA Helen did a brilliant job of making me feel better.

'Don't worry about it, kid,' said Pete, giving my shoulder a squeeze. 'Today's news is tomorrow's fish and chip paper.'

And he was right of course. No one gave me a hard time about the affair – everyone, including Mum and Dad, just wanted to make sure I was OK. I was worried there might be a backlash from our fans but there wasn't, and I was really grateful for that.

One day Reece and I bumped into Bonnie and a friend when we were out shopping at the Bentall Centre in Kingston, Surrey. We were walking around holding hands and she spotted us. She came up behind us and started ranting and raving in the middle of the food court; then she slapped Reece in the face and screamed at me, 'Do you want to meet my child?' It was horrendous.

Reece stayed with his sister Tara while I was in America. Understandably, he wasn't in a good place at that point and he ended up taking everything out on me. He started by saying I should be investigating our management in case they were ripping us off. I think it was just his way of feeling involved.

Another blow for Reece had been that, at the beginning of the year, the record company had found out we were seeing each other. As it was really frowned on to date one of the artists, all the good acts such as The Backstreet Boys and Britney had been taken away from him. He was head of promotions at the time, so it was a big demotion and he felt he had no choice but to leave.

Reece got a job with Warner Music Group and had to do a bit of travelling to America, so he was able to come out for at bit of the tour, but I was busy working a lot of the time – we kicked off the tour in July and were away for nearly three months.

When Reece was back home in London we spoke on the phone every day, but nine times out of ten I'd end up crying because I was finding it so hard being away from him. I also felt guilty about not being at home with him, especially after what he'd just been through with Bonnie, and I knew how upset he was about leaving Olivia.

Just as we jetted off to the States to support Britney, we released 'Love's Got A Hold On My Heart' – the first single from our next album *Steptacular*, which was due for release in the autumn. The single made it to number two, but missed out on the number-one slot thanks to Ricky Martin's 'Livin' La Vida Loca'. There just always seemed to be a bigger record keeping us off that top spot!

We joined the Britney tour in New York because the label wanted us to reshoot the video for 'One For Sorrow' as it was going to be in a Melissa Joan Hart film that was part of our American promotion. Following on from that we did a few dates in Canada, then picked up a tour bus and started touring around America. We didn't do the whole of Britney's tour, but we did a big chunk of it.

Britney was just a kid – only seventeen years old – and we didn't spend that much time with her. The indoor arenas are truly enormous in the States – far bigger than they are in the UK – and the backstage areas are vast, so there weren't many opportunities to socialize with her. She was very sweet, though, and I remember her coming into catering one day with Justin Timberlake, before it came out that they were seeing each other.

H got to know her a bit better because he ended up travelling on her private jet a few times, which didn't go down well at all with the rest of the band!

When we had started the tour, our management had booked us flights from each city to the next, but they'd also got us a sleeper bus. Lisa, Lee, Faye and I decided to cancel about fifteen flights each to claw back some of the money we'd spent on the tour: the travel costs were coming out of our royalty account, and we didn't see the point in expensive flights when we could take the tour bus. We were also going to be charged for reshooting the video for 'One For Sorrow', which we didn't want to do. The record company was funding the whole trip to America, so that money would have to be recouped as well.

But H refused to do it. He's never been able to sleep very well and he wouldn't sleep on the bus. I think the rest of us felt his behaviour was a little diva-ish and it definitely drove a bit of a wedge between him and us. I couldn't understand it because I don't think we ever spent the entire night in the bus on any journey. We'd mostly be offstage by eight o'clock and we'd get straight into the bus. It was usually a five- or six-hour drive, but we'd be at our next hotel and in bed by 2 a.m. at the very latest. H wouldn't budge, though, so he either flew by himself or with Britney and her assistant.

I didn't fall out with H on that trip, but I suppose I was spending less time with him. Up until then, Lisa and I had never been that close because we didn't have much in common, but on that trip we became the best of friends. She'd met her future husband, Johnny Shentall, by this point, and I think she understood now how I felt about Reece.

Although it was nice to feel closer with Lisa, I didn't enjoy most of the tour. Whenever I travelled with Steps I felt bloody miserable quite a lot of the time because I was away from Reece. I'd usually take myself off to my room so I could be alone, so I didn't go out with the rest of the band much at all; we might have been in the most amazing place in the world, but I just wanted to be at home with Reece.

Before Steps hit it really big, I remember going to a beautiful island resort in Singapore where I spent the entire time thinking about what time it was back in the UK and whether or not I'd be able to speak to Reece. Then I'd start worrying about whether he'd pick up the phone because he might be at home with Bonnie. All I thought about was speaking to him! I never allowed myself to have a good time and I didn't make the most of every situation. I should have enjoyed myself more! Steps saw the world, but I just saw the inside of lots of different hotel rooms.

But I didn't quite know how to handle the situation I'd found myself in. If I think about it now, I was only nineteen when I joined Steps, and when I'd left school I'd gone straight into TSD. I'd never lived away from my parents or had a proper long-term relationship. The rest of the band had either lived with a partner or lived away from home – they'd had a bit of life experience. But apart from Saturday jobs and a few months of temp work, all I knew about was being in a pop group and going on tour.

It didn't help that by the time of the Britney tour, I was feeling a little bit isolated from the rest of the band. It was uncomfortable knowing that they weren't happy about the fact I'd been getting more vocals than they were, even though they never said anything to me directly. While the rest of the group didn't sing on every record, I did, although there was always someone else on the track with me – either Faye, or H, or Faye and Lisa. But I was the only one who sang on everything and I guess my voice is quite prominent in the choruses.

To add to the tension, Steve Jenkins, the head of our record company, joined us in LA to play us the new album *Steptacular*. Just like Pete Waterman had done with *Step One*, Steve played us the whole thing through from beginning to end; then played what would be our next single. It was 'After The Love Has Gone' – the only track off the album that I'd sung on my own. I couldn't believe it – it was like history repeating itself!

No one said anything to me – not even H this time. Once again, they just got up and walked out, although I'm sure they were straight on the phone to our management.

I suppose I consciously isolated myself a bit from the others, too. I'm not the kind of person who needs to be

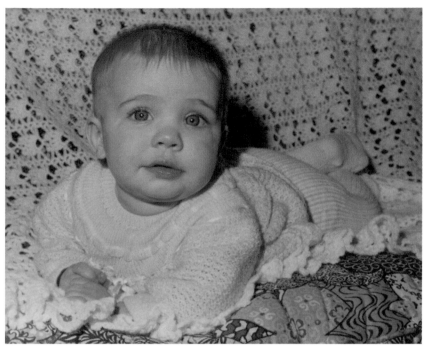

This is me about seven months old. No sign yet that I'm really Elvis reincarnated!

Above With my sister Gemma on holiday.

Left Taken in June 1981, when I'm almost four.

Putting on a little show for my parents, who'd be treated to songs like 'Over the Rainbow' and 'The Sun Will Come Out Tomorrow'.

The Sindy Swingers! Melanie is on guitar, Hayley is singing, Gemma is on keyboard and I'm playing a mean recorder.

Above With Melanie, my childhood best friend.

Right I joined a running club just before starting secondary school, but you can see I hated taking part in competitions like this!

From the programme for
The Sound of Music – my
first lead role.

With Cossie and Bonnie, all of us
looking so excited to be in TSD.

I loved my year spent touring with TSD. Bonnie is in the middle and Cossie is on the right.

Left The photograph I sent in, along with my tape, for the Steps audition.

Below In 1998, when this photo was taken, things had started to take off for Steps in a big way.

Right My twenty-first birthday party! With Mum, Dad and Gemma.

Below right With Reece in January 1999. We have always been soulmates.

Below far right On stage for our first arena tour, in 1999. The stress of my relationship with Reece, as well as tensions surfacing in the band, meant my weight started to drop during this time.

All together at the Brits in March 2000 – we'd won an award for best live act.
I had only recently split from Reece, and look horribly thin.

Above left Reece managed to spend some time with me in America during the Britney tour in 1999.

Left With Faye at the Fox Teen Awards, during our Britney tour. Look at my outfit – what was I thinking?!

By summer 2000 Mark and I had fallen into a relationship.

Above left On the Steptacular
tour in 2000.

Above right This was our last show,
Wembley, 22 December 2001, the day
after H and I resigned. I was crying all
the way through, especially at the
beginning and the end.

Right With one of my best
friends, Jackie, who was also
my make-up artist.

with other people all the time: I'm quite happy with my own company and I liked to relax on tour by lying on my bed listening to music. I don't think the others really understood that, and they probably thought I was being unsociable or stroppy.

I did go out occasionally, though, and I remember we attended the Fox Teen Awards while we were on the Britney tour. We were there to present Britney with an award, but no one knew who the hell we were! And I looked ridiculous – I was wearing a very short, red crop top with white trousers and a massive cowboy hat that was far too big for me.

It was a bizarre experience because it seemed like everyone who was anyone in Hollywood was there – it was wall-to-wall movie stars. At one point I had to squeeze past Sandra Bullock in a doorway, and later I found myself standing next to J.Lo and thinking, 'I so don't belong here!' It was a rare showbiz night out for me.

H was seeing our manager Tim Byrne on the US tour. I'd known about it for a couple of months, but none of the others had been told. I'd already guessed something was going on between the two of them before H told me about their relationship – I'd spotted a few clues, and he and Tim were always getting dropped off together: Tim had a house in Ealing and H lived in Acton, but in reality their houses were about a minute round the corner from each other. Then one day, H had sent me a text message that was meant for Tim and that's how I found out for definite. H was a bit embarrassed and annoyed with himself, but he took me out for a drink and told me about his relationship with Tim; I think they were both a bit relieved that someone knew. H asked me to keep it a secret from the others and I said I would.

A really big deal has been made about me spilling the beans to the others, but they'd already guessed that H and Tim were an item and used to speculate about it all the time. Then, one day towards the end of the trip, I was in a shopping mall with Faye and Lisa. They came right out and asked me, and I just didn't want to lie any more.

'OK, if I tell you, please don't tell H and Tim because it will cause so much trouble but, yes, they are seeing each other,' I said.

'Don't worry, we won't say anything,' they both assured me.

When we got back to the hotel later on, the girls told Lee and I begged them all again not to reveal that they knew. They promised they wouldn't. Thankfully, the rest of the tour went on without anything being said.

Pretty much as soon as we got back from the States we started rehearsing for 'The Next Step' arena tour, which was due to kick off in Sheffield in October.

One night we had a band meeting at the LWT rehearsal studios in Oval. We were all sitting round in a big circle talking about the tour and other business when Tim asked if there was anything else we'd like to talk about.

Lee came right out and asked Tim and H if they were in a relationship – he'd obviously been stewing on it since the US tour.

'It doesn't matter if you are seeing each other, but we want you to be honest about it,' he said.

H and Tim were taken by surprise and clearly didn't know how to respond, throwing each other confused looks. They didn't admit it though, which frustrated Lee, who then let slip that someone had told him they were a couple.

I couldn't believe what I was hearing. I was shaking and kept telling myself, 'Don't cry, everyone's here, don't cry.' I was terrified of getting found out.

After the meeting, Reece picked me up and I remember getting home and crying myself to sleep because I was so worried H would find out it was me who'd told everyone. What was unfair was that I knew everyone had already worked it out by themselves and that all I did was confirm it for them, but I didn't think H would see it that way.

The next day we had to appear on the Saturday morning kids' show *SM:TV*. In the dressing room afterwards, Lee was insistent that H and Tim told the truth.

'Until this is sorted out, until someone comes clean, I'm not coming back to rehearsals,' he said, then he pointed at me and H and added, 'You two had better go and have a conversation about who's right.'

I could not believe it. Lee had completely and utterly dropped me in it, even though I'd begged all of them to keep me out of it. They'd all agreed – in fact, they'd promised they wouldn't say anything.

I had to sit and have a really uncomfortable conversation with H. I tried to explain that the others had already guessed he was seeing Tim, but I'm not sure he believed me and, after that, our relationship was strained. Rehearsals were pretty awkward, too – H tried to keep up appearances but, gradually, he began to resent me more and more, and he started to shut me out so we stopped being as close. At that point I think H hated me. Yes, I admit it wasn't my secret to tell, but somehow the whole situation became my fault and I got the blame for everything – from Lee, Lisa and Faye, and from H and Tim, because I'd opened the can of worms.

The others seemed fine with H, though. 'Why did you have to keep it a secret?' was what Lee kept asking.

I completely understood the rest of the band was unhappy Tim and H had kept this from them for the past two years, and I think they felt it threw a whole new light on the dynamics of the group because one of us had been dating our manager. But I couldn't understand why the blame was being laid at my door. I felt totally as if I had been stabbed in the back, and it meant I began to feel even more isolated from the rest of the band. I even said to Reece at the time, 'That's it, I'm done with Lee.' It was a huge deal for me.

*

Despite the bad feeling among us, though, things were going from strength to strength for the band. Our second album *Steptacular* was released on 24 October 1999 to coincide with the arena tour, and it shot straight to number one. We also released our first single of the new album – 'After The Love Has Gone', which got to number five.

Around that time we also launched dolls of the band at a toy fair in London. There was a big photo call, with dozens of photographers – as we'd become more successful, the national press had started to take more of an interest in us – clamouring to get shots of us.

I remember sitting behind a desk, and nearly all of the paparazzi were shouting my name and practically standing on top of each other to get a photo: 'Let's get a picture, Claire. Stand over here, Claire!' I was a bit surprised, thinking, 'Gosh, it must be my turn to be the favourite,' but then forgot about it. The next morning, however, I realized with horror why they'd all been shouting my name – the tabloids had printed stories saying I was pregnant because my stomach wasn't as flat as it used to be. The photographers had obviously been told to get a picture of me looking pregnant.

I felt absolutely shit, really horrible. If you're a woman, there's nothing worse than someone asking, 'When's the baby due?' when you're not pregnant. I was only twenty-two and, given how self-conscious I'd become about my figure since joining Steps, I felt absolutely devastated. I think it was the time of the month, so my tummy was bloated, because I certainly wasn't eating much at the time. Those pictures set me off again into starvation mode and I remember thinking, 'That's it, I can't eat.'

If you're in the public eye, you're expected to be really thick-skinned and not take any notice of stories like that, but it's hard not to when you're young and have a completely screwed-up body image. It's no surprise there are so many girls in the industry with eating disorders because there's too much pressure to look a certain way. I'm sick of hearing celebrities saying their skinny bodies are natural – no, they're bloody not! The majority of them are skinny because they hardly eat. I know because I've been there.

It was probably the first time my weight was written about, but it certainly wouldn't be the last.

As well as dealing with the fallout from the H and Tim revelations, and the frosty atmosphere at rehearsals, my relationship with Reece wasn't going well, either. When I returned home from America things were OK for a while, but then we began to argue a lot. The situation with Bonnie and Olivia continued to be difficult and I sometimes found it all overwhelming.

Reece would often say, 'Do you want to meet Olivia?' but I'd always make excuses not to see her, partly because it didn't feel right given what I imagined Bonnie's feelings might be. It was also because I knew, deep inside, that meeting Olivia would make her real to me and then I wouldn't be able to bury the pain of Reece having a baby with another woman. I bought her presents and asked about her, but I never spent any time with her as a baby.

Reece also started to complain that I wasn't around enough and we argued about that. He needed me to be there, but nearly all of my time was taken up with Steps and I had absolutely no control over my schedule. He was still living with Tara in Wimbledon – miles away from me in Uxbridge – and Olivia was around, too, which meant it began to get more and more difficult to see each other.

If I'm honest, though, once our affair was out in the open the relationship felt different – suddenly it seemed serious and grown-up, and not something I felt able to cope with at twenty-two. It just didn't feel like it had when we were having the affair. I wanted Reece to be the same as he was when we were sneaking around stealing kisses while no one was looking and making plans for liaisons in hotel rooms and, of course, he couldn't. The situation had changed. He was ten years older than I was, with a young baby and an ex who wasn't making things easy for him.

Around that time I finally put the wheels in motion to get a place of my own. I'd spotted a house for sale in the next road to where my parents lived and I was quite excited about it. It was a dump, but I could see the potential and I had lots of plans to do it up. I took Reece to see it and he told me I was mad for buying it. I just felt as if he was criticizing everything I did at that point and that he wasn't being supportive.

It was a very vulnerable time in my relationship with Reece and that's when a dancer called Mark Webb entered the scene.

I'd actually met him briefly earlier that year. At the time he was dating another dancer who was working for one of our support acts on the theatre tour we did and had come to visit her at the gig in Wolverhampton.

'Nice to meet you, Faye,' were his first words to me.

'Er, nice to meet you, too, but I'm not Faye!' I shot back, thinking he seemed a bit cocky.

It wasn't a good start but when he was hired as one of the dancers on 'The Next Step' arena tour we got to know each other at rehearsals. He was three years older than me, a blond surfer type with a fit and muscular body. He was also a very good dancer and very sure of himself. Everyone liked Mark – he was a really friendly guy and we clicked and had a laugh together. I didn't really notice that he spent a lot of time hanging around me, although I do remember he offered me his coat when we were doing production rehearsals for our opening show in Sheffield because I was complaining about the cold. The rest of the band were winking at me and teasing me about it, but I didn't think anything of it at the time.

Gradually, though, as the tour went on, we began spending a bit more time together. I really liked him, but I kept trying to convince myself I didn't. I was always looking for reasons not to fancy him – 'He's a bit short' or 'I don't like his hair' or 'He's too stocky.'

Meanwhile, things between Reece and I weren't getting any better. When we first got together I used to joke it was just our timing that was wrong and that we'd meet up again when we were both in our sixties and get married. Now, it didn't seem so much like a joke. Things just felt complicated and messy, and the relationship wasn't turning out as I'd expected it to. If I'd been older, with more experience of life, I would have tried harder to work through it. As you get older you realize all relationships encounter bumps in the road, but you can get over them with a bit of hard work and patience. At that point in my life, though, all I remember thinking was, 'This isn't my fairy tale any more.'

5

THE END OF THE FAIRY TALE

'Good evening, Wembley!'

They were the words I'd been waiting my whole life to say and now, on 4 November 1999, I was saying them to a packed arena. As I looked out across the sea of screaming Steps fans I felt so overcome with emotion I had to stop myself from bursting into tears. It was the moment I thought, 'Whoa, this really is it now, we've made it.'

I was beyond excited on the run up to the Wembley show. It was extra special for me because it was on my home turf and I'd worked there as a kid. The dream I'd cherished as a teenager to sing on that stage was about to come true, and I knew that very few people are lucky enough to get that chance.

When we had arrived at Wembley earlier that day, the girls had been given the star dressing room. Next to my place at the mirror was a steward's polo shirt with a note from the lady who managed the stewards saying, '*I remember you, Claire. You used to say that one day you'd be up on that stage and I always knew you would be. Oh, and the briefing's at six o'clock!'*

Whenever I tell that story it still makes me cry. I couldn't believe she'd remembered me. It had been six or seven years since I'd left my job there and I was incredibly touched by her gesture. That evening, when I looked down to the stewards from the stage, I thought, 'I can't believe I'm actually up here!'

The show started with a carnival theme and we made our entrance through the audience disguised in masks and cloaks with minders walking either side of us. When we got up on stage, our disguises were stripped off to reveal our costumes – mine was a pair of yellow hipsters and a sequinned bra.

The show opened with 'Love's Got A Hold On My Heart'. When the intro music started I got really choked again and had to force myself to hold it together because I didn't want to start blubbing on stage!

By the time we'd got to Wembley we knew the show really well and we were comfortable with it. It was an amazing experience and one I'll never forget. We'd only been out there as Steps for a couple of years and we were already playing sell-out shows at Wembley Arena – it was hard to take in.

It's impossible to express the buzz you get from doing a show like that and it's hard to replace when you come off tour – it's addictive. Getting the opportunity to sing for all those people who loved our music was all I ever cared about – I wasn't bothered about the fame, once I'd experienced it; and I certainly had no time for the band politics. I just loved the singing. But the tours, especially the arena tour, really catapulted us into the big league – we were the star attraction now!

We did five nights at Wembley and on one of the days, Reece and I managed to have sex in the dressing room! It was quite early in the day, so no one else was there and we locked the dressing room door, then went into the bathroom and locked that door, too, just to be on the safe side. It's one happy memory I have from that time but in truth, things were going from bad to worse as far as our relationship was concerned. On top of our other problems my schedule was unrelenting and now that Reece wasn't working for Jive any more, it meant we barely got to see each other. We'd started to drift apart and, towards the end of the tour, I was thinking, 'I don't want to be in this any more.'

Mark was also giving me a lot of attention at the time – in fact he chased me pretty hard – and, as the tour had gone on, we'd begun to get closer. We didn't sleep together, but we had a kiss one night and he did sleep in my room a few times. Mark was appealing at the time because he was a light-hearted distraction from what was going on with Reece: with Mark I felt like a twenty-two-year-old again.

*

In mid-December we travelled to Ireland for the last leg of the tour and Reece came over to visit. We had a really big row over something, but we made up before he flew home. The first night I got back to London, however, I went to see him at his sister's house and that's when we split up. It was only a few days before Christmas.

When I'd gone over there that evening I actually hadn't intended on ending the relationship, but once again we got into an argument. We'd always talked about getting married in the future, and now Reece brought it up again.

'Claire,' he said, sounding strained, 'do you still want to marry me?'

'No,' I heard myself saying. 'Not with the way things are at the moment.'

It escalated from there and we talked, cried and argued all night about everything we'd been through since we'd started our affair. Nothing was resolved. Reece ended up making me open my Christmas present – he'd bought me a diamond solitaire necklace that I'd wanted for ages. It was beautiful and my eyes filled with tears as I looked at it because I knew this was the end for us.

I told him I didn't want to be with him any more and, early the next morning, I left in a cab, feeling emotionally and physically drained. I had a bin bag full of my stuff and my big 'subs bench coat' as Reece called it – it was a long duvet coat like the one footballers wear on the subs bench. I couldn't quite believe it was happening, even as I gave him a last kiss goodbye.

That day I had to do the *Top Of The Pops* Christmas special – we were performing our new single, which was a cover of Kylie Minogue's 'Better The Devil You Know'. It was another double A-side along with 'Say You'll Be Mine', and stormed into the charts at number four. I'd just split up with the love of my life, but I had to get out on that stage, put on my game face and plaster on a big beaming smile. I did it – wearing devil horns and everything – even though I felt a complete wreck inside. That day I should have been going to see a flat with Reece, which he was thinking of buying. He had been hoping I'd like it enough to move in with him. It was hard to get my head around the fact that our future together had disappeared.

When I had left his sister's house that morning, I knew I couldn't see him or speak to him again because, if I did, we would have got back together, just like all those times before when we were having the affair. I honestly believed our relationship wasn't right at that time, that I was doing what was best for both of us, but walking away was absolutely bloody awful.

Reece rang my mum and dad's house all the time over that Christmas, but I refused to speak to him. My dad threatened him with all sorts, saying, 'Don't ever ring here again!' It was a horrible time and I know Reece felt I'd ruined Olivia's first birthday for him.

Mark was still on the scene and I'd convinced myself I wanted to be with him. So, after I ended things with Reece, I visited Mark in Leicester over the holidays and that was the first time we slept together. But although Mark was sweet, I ended it at the beginning of the new year because it just didn't feel right. I'd fallen into dating him on the rebound and my heart wasn't in it. I didn't want to be with anyone because I still loved Reece, and fancied him like crazy, and knew I needed time to get over him.

After that, I kept Mark at arm's length and it wasn't until we started rehearsing in the spring for our next tour that anything happened between us again.

I was still really thin at this point. I probably wasn't being quite so strict about my diet, but then I'd go through periods of starving myself, then relaxing a bit more. If I had something 'bad' like a burger or a cake, I'd eat practically nothing the following day to make up for it: for a long time that's how I used to control my weight. For a while I was eating nothing but rice cakes every day – I'd just eat them straight from the packet because they filled me up and contained hardly any calories. I'd pretty much stopped exercising – I'd go through periods of sitting on the bike at the gym, but I'd always be reading a book or a magazine instead of working out properly.

In February, *Steps To The Stars* – our very own talent show – went out on CBBC. Someone at the BBC had come to our management with the idea and wanted me and H to be the hosts, and for Steps to perform a song at the end of each show. Three acts performed, then viewers would phone in and vote for their favourite – kind of like *X Factor* but on a much smaller scale! The series winner then got to perform on the Saturday kids' TV show *Live & Kicking* and to spend a day with Steps. Gareth Gates, who later found fame on *Pop Idol*, was a contestant and so was McFly's Danny Jones, who was in a band called Y2K with his sister and a mate.

Inevitably it caused angst in the band because H and I had been asked to host the show: Faye, Lisa and Lee were only required to turn up for a couple of days to film all the Steps performances that were shown at the end of each programme, so it was really awkward. The others told our management they were unhappy with the situation, although they never said anything to us. The good thing was that H and I started to get on a bit better again and we had a laugh making the show with all its fluff-ups and out-takes.

In March 2000, Steps won a Brit Award for Best Live Act, which was pretty exciting because, although we'd been nominated the year before for Best British Newcomer and performed at the show, we hadn't won anything. As well as winning Best Live Act, we'd also been nominated for Best Selling British Live Act and Best British Pop Act – we were on fire!

It wasn't long after I'd split up from Reece and he was still working for Warners, so I knew he was going to be at the awards show in Earls Court. I was terrified of bumping into him. To make matters worse, I didn't have a date or a friend with me that night: Lee had just broken up with a friend of mine, who I was meant to be taking as my guest, and he didn't want her to come because he was taking his new girlfriend. So I ended up sitting on my own at our table while everyone else had their partners with them.

It was freezing cold that night and I was wearing leather trousers with a leather bikini bra and a flimsy beaded shawl, which was never going to keep me warm. All I did was sit there and panic that I was going to bump into Reece, thinking up scenarios about what would happen if I did: would he start a row? Would I start crying? So, once again, when I should have been having the time of my life and enjoying our success, I was sitting there worrying about Reece – it was the story of my life!

I said to the others, 'If you see Reece coming over here, please warn me.' And, of course, he did come over, but he just gave me a lovely smile, leaned in and whispered in my ear, 'You look beautiful.'

He walked away and that was it.

I nearly had a heart attack! I spent about five minutes trying to get the lid off a bottle of vodka that was in a bucket next to our table, not realizing the lid was already off it and that I had cut my hand to ribbons.

Afterwards, we went to the Spice Girls after-party at a West End club called Sugar Reef. J Brown from the boy band Five was there. I'd managed to drink enough vodka by then to decide that, not only did I quite fancy him, but it would be a good idea to spend the rest of the night walking past him, trying to get his attention. He wasn't interested, though, and ended up going off with Mel C.

Katie Price and her boyfriend Dane Bowers from boy

band Another Level were also there, and I remember her being a bit funny with all the girls because she was obviously worried they'd all be trying it on with Dane! I knew Dane from the music scene so I said hello, but all I remember about Katie was that she was wearing a cowboy hat and had a very firm handshake!

Being pretty drunk and newly single, I stayed until the bitter end, clutching our Brit, while the others trotted sensibly off to bed. By then I was telling anyone I bumped into that I'd had money nicked out of my bag because all my cash had gone, only to realize later that I'd been buying rounds at the bar all night.

I only had about an hour's sleep as I had to get up at the crack of dawn to appear on *SM:TV* and to perform 'Deeper Shade Of Blue', which was to be our next single. I'm sure I smelled like a brewery – I must have had alcohol oozing out of every pore and the worst hangover in the world!

That morning Geri Halliwell was at *SM:TV*, too. It was after she'd left the Spice Girls and she'd performed solo at the Brits the previous night, causing a storm by emerging from a giant pair of inflatable legs for her performance! She's absolutely tiny and I remember her looking up at me for ages with a quizzical expression on her face before saying, 'You're really quite pretty, aren't you?' That was all she said to me. She seemed surprised that I didn't have a face like the back end of a bus! I wasn't quite sure if I should take it as a compliment or an insult.

I'd met the Spice Girls once before in the canteen at the

studio for *Top Of The Pops* and was most struck by how unhappy Posh looked. I'd thought, 'How can you be that miserable with all your money AND David Beckham?' I was always a bit too shy and awestruck to strike up conversations, though.

Top Of The Pops was a good place for star spotting. Robbie Williams came into the make-up room once and, after chatting to us all, started singing to everyone. I can't remember what he really sang but I like to think it was 'Angels'. H also reckons Robbie advised him to leave Steps when he saw him sitting in the corridor at *Top Of The Pops* looking miserable. Apparently he came over to H and said, 'I think it's time to leave, isn't it?'

Probably the best *Top of The Pops* moment for me was standing in the studio watching Madonna rehearse 'Frozen'. She was a proper superstar. No one could get anywhere near her, so we didn't get to meet her, but a guy from her management company got her album signed for me – that was good enough for me!

After the highs of the Brits, I found out that Reece was seeing a French girl who worked at his new record company. I felt really upset about it. I knew that I was the one who'd left him, and I'd had a fling with Mark, but I'd soon realized how much I still loved Reece and ended things. Now I kept thinking, 'How can you be going out with someone already when you were supposed to love me so much?' It had only been a couple of months since we'd broken up and I admit I sent him a few arsey text messages saying I couldn't believe he was already dating another woman. We ended up having a few rows via text, although we never spoke on the phone.

I tried to take my mind of it by concentrating on the rehearsals for our next arena tour, which were already underway by April. We were riding high on the success of our platinum-selling album *Steptacular*, and the last single, 'Deeper Shade Of Blue', had made it to number four in the charts. The 'Steptacular' tour was another sell-out, with thirty-one dates booked around the country.

Mark was one of our dancers on that tour and, at first, things were a bit frosty between us. He wouldn't talk to me for a while, but we did eventually become friends again. It was clear he wanted a relationship with me, but I was happy on my own at that point and was adamant I wouldn't go out with him.

Mark was friendly with Lisa and her boyfriend Johnny so he came down to visit them one night during that rehearsal period and we all went out for dinner. The cheeky bugger expected to stay the night at my house afterwards, but I wasn't having any of it! I was determined nothing was going to happen.

After Reece and I had split up, I'd started going out with my friends a lot more and tried to forget about men for a while: we used to go to a club called Titanic most week-ends and get very drunk. I think it was good for me – I needed to do it.

One night I fell off a chair in the bar and landed right on my coccyx; it bloody hurt! The club called an ambulance but I thought they were making too much fuss and, being the worse for wear, flatly refused to get into it. Instead Myleene Klass's husband, Graham Quinn, who did Steps' security at the time and who was out socializing with a couple of the lads from Boyzone, wheeled me out of the back entrance of the club in an office chair so I could get in a cab to Hillingdon Hospital! No damage was done and I was very sheepish when my mum came to pick us up from casualty at 6 a.m.

The tour kicked off in Glasgow in May. Midway through it I caved in and ended up going out with Mark one night.

I thought he looked a bit different that day and I decided I quite fancied him, so we started seeing each other again. We just kind of fell into it, I suppose. One night, we went out to the 10 Room nightclub in London for Shelina's birthday and I got absolutely plastered. I felt so dizzy and ill I had to hunker down on some bridge over the Thames, then suddenly I was leaning over the side to puke into the river – that's how drunk I was! I was lucky no one was around to see me make such an arse of myself – these days you'd never get away with it because there would be a dozen paparazzi chasing you down the street and the pictures would be all over the papers the next day, or you'd be snapped on a camera phone and the image uploaded to Twitter!

When I got home, I had a bit of a moment when Mark

was putting me to bed and I just thought, 'Oh, I think I love you!' It was the drink talking, of course, and I wish I'd never said it out loud because after that I found myself in a proper relationship with him.

Although I did care about him, right from the off there were signs that the relationship probably wasn't going to last – if only I'd paid attention to them. For one thing, that summer, on my twenty-third birthday, Mark had my initial tattooed on his arm. Even then, instead of thinking what a sweet gesture it was, I just thought, 'What a stupid thing to do!'

Meanwhile, relationships in the band weren't improving. Faye and I were getting on well at the time, but H still hadn't really forgiven me for telling the others about his relationship with Tim. During rehearsals he'd sometimes get angry with me and, once the tour got underway, things between me and H deteriorated further.

Towards the end of the tour we had decided to put on an extra matinee performance at Wembley because we wanted to film it for a DVD. I was told there was no rush to be back for the matinee – unlike the evening shows when you had to be on stage bang on time or you'd get charged for going over – and I could get ready in my own time.

None of us were ready, except for H, but he chose to march into my dressing room and start ranting and raving at me.

He always used to be ready way before any of the rest of us – an hour before going on stage he'd be there with his head mic on, pacing up and down the corridor going over his links. I'd just think, 'Come off it!' and leave him to it. But he was really unhappy this day and I'll never forget he snapped at me, 'The world doesn't revolve around your arse, Claire!' then stormed off.

I started crying and our make-up artist Jackie was trying to make me feel better, and saying, 'Please don't cry, you've got all your make-up on!' It was full-on stage make-up, which she then had to retouch, and that made us even later.

As H and Lee were leaving the dressing room, I walked up behind them and slammed the door, accidentally catching Lee. I didn't hurt him, but it was definitely Lee I got with the door and not H, even though it had been for his benefit! I had to pop my head out the door and say sorry. Tensions were boiling over and nerves were frayed.

Because I was seeing Mark by then, and Shelina was also on tour with us, I spent most of my time with them and the rest of the dancers so I rarely socialized with the band. Because of the success we'd had, we always had dancers with us whenever we did TV shows, so I always had plenty of friends around.

By that point I think everyone had got a bit carried away with the fame side of things. Everything we did was successful – after '5, 6, 7 8', all our singles had shot straight into the Top 10, nothing ever failed, and hits became par for the course. It was no surprise to us when another arena tour was a sell-out – there was no reason to think it wouldn't be. It's hard not to be affected by that kind of success – you begin to think you're invincible and start believing your own hype. None of us was perfect. Every one of us in the band had our moments when a diva-like streak would emerge – even me! Rather than filter my reaction to something, I behaved a bit like a spoilt kid sometimes, and if I was asked to get up early to do some PR or to turn up at an industry event, I'd often say something like, 'Arrgh, do I *really* have to?' My reluctance to do things probably came across as stroppy, although I thought I was perfect at the time! I'd never behave like that now – in fact, I probably spend my time overcompensating to ensure people don't think I'm a diva. I like to think I've redeemed myself since!

By now, we'd all started to live much more separate lives – when we weren't working together we didn't speak to each other at all. We didn't meet up or even talk on the phone. When we had a break over Christmas, we would say goodbye and see each other in two weeks. I suppose when you spend that much time with people you don't kiss each other hello and goodbye every day: it was like waking up in the morning and going down to breakfast and seeing your family sitting there.

On tour, everyone had their own alliances, and their friends would come to visit. Faye was with her boyfriend Jasper – who became her first husband – Lisa was with Johnny, H and Tim were still together and Lee had a girlfriend, too. Unless we were rehearsing or on stage, we barely spent any time together at all.

While the rest of the band started to make friends with

other celebrities, all my good friends were among the people we worked with – from the record company, and behind the scenes on our tours. I would always be the one sitting and chatting with the crew, the dancers or the wardrobe lady – those were the people who I felt comfortable with. Even now, my best friends are the people we worked with then: our old tour manager, John Procter; Jackie; and Shelina. They were my unit, I suppose, and when the band broke up, they never went away. They stayed and supported me and made sure I was all right.

I was never into the sex, drugs and rock 'n' roll side of things on tour: as far as the sex went, I've still only slept with two men and I married them both. Someone once said to me, 'There are two types of girls: the kind you sleep with and the kind you marry', and I'm obviously the kind you marry! There are a lot of people in this business who just want to have a 'bit of fun', but I think guys just knew they weren't going to get that from me. I must just have one of those faces.

When it comes to drugs, I don't ever remember being offered anything, apart from once in a club. I was standing minding my own business when someone said to me, 'Are you sorted?' I didn't have a clue what he was talking about until a friend explained that's what people say to you when they're asking if you want to buy drugs! Drugs never inter-ested me for one second, though – I've always been pretty anti them. Growing up, I had a couple of friends who had had their drinks spiked and it really frightened me. Plus when

I was eighteen, I was really affected by the Leah Betts story – she was the teenager who died just after her eighteenth birthday after taking Ecstasy. I also remember reading the *Sweet Valley High* books and one of the major characters tried cocaine and had a heart attack and died. It always stuck in my head that it could happen to me. As I've already said, I'm not a big risk-taker and I also don't like the thought of feeling out of control on drugs, so they just weren't for me.

I've no doubt that drug taking was probably going on around me, but I was oblivious to it and, even if I'd been talking to someone who was on drugs, I'd never have known. I'd probably have just assumed they were drunk or a bit odd!

After the 'Steptacular' tour finished, we went to New York for a couple of weeks in August to record some tracks for our next album *Buzz*, which was due for release in the autumn. The songs we recorded there were awful – the worst we'd ever done. It was the first time we'd recorded outside of PWL and it felt like the tracks had been written for a US artist and rejected. One of them – 'Happy Go Lucky' – was really similar to a Britney song, but not nearly as good. I felt the quality of the songs was poor compared to what we'd already done.

There was a producer we worked with there who really looked like Reece and I got a little bit obsessed with him. One evening we all went out, and I got chatting to him. After getting back to my hotel room that night I decided to go out again to try to find his hotel, but ended up in Times Square not knowing where the hell I was! Although I was going out with Mark at the time, it seemed Reece was never far from my thoughts.

When we got back home, our next single, 'Summer Of Love'/'When I Said Goodbye', was released in July and it made it to number five. Our schedule was as packed as ever. We also had outdoor gigs planned throughout July and August, including one at Hyde Park in London.

Reece was there with a support band called Point Break. He had brought along his French girlfriend and I felt crazy with jealousy. 'How dare he bring his girlfriend to my gig!' I snapped after he'd come over to say hello when I was sat backstage with my family.

Just after that gig, Mark and I managed to squeeze in a holiday to Mauritius. While I was there, I had a text row with Reece, which started with what I thought was his insensitive behaviour at the gig but became about all the hurt we both still felt over the past. Mark didn't have a clue we were texting each other – I kept making excuses to go back to the room so I could look at my phone.

That summer I finally moved out of my parents' house and into my own, newly refurbished place around the corner, and I had a party there for my twenty-third birthday. Although the house had been ready to move into three weeks before, that was the first night I slept there and, even after I moved in, I still went round to Mum and Dad's every night for my dinner. Moving out was a gradual process – as much as I wanted to live on my own and be an adult, I still felt I needed the protection my family gave me.

Mark started living with me by accident, really. He'd been travelling up and down from Leicester all the time and didn't have a base in London, so I gave him a key and he was pretty much there all the time after that.

We also went to Sweden to record more tracks for *Buzz* – 'It's The Way You Make Me Feel' and 'Here & Now'. The control had been taken away from Pete Waterman a little bit at that stage and we felt ready to try something new. The big thing at the time was to record in Sweden – other acts on our label, including Britney, NSYNC and the Backstreet Boys had all worked with Swedish record producers Max Martin and Andreas Carlsson and we wanted to do the same.

It was when we were recording *Buzz* that the plan was made to start giving us all an equal amount of vocals. I was a bit annoyed that such a big deal was being made out of it, as if I'd deliberately hogged all the limelight before: I'd only sung 'One For Sorrow' and 'After The Love Has Gone' all the way through on my own. At the beginning, Faye and I used to sing the lead vocals and sometimes Lisa would sing the middle eight or the verse at the end – but it was always me *with* someone else.

While we were in Sweden, Lee had a row with Tim over two lines he was meant to be singing on his own. I was asked to double the vocals so I went in, recorded the lines in ten minutes and came back out again. Lee wasn't happy at all and he started to argue with Tim about it. Lee remembers this completely differently to me, but I remember him saying, 'Why is she singing over my bit? If it was in my key and a different style I'd piss all over the song.'

I was stunned at his reaction.

'I can't believe you just said that! Even if it was in your key I'd still sing it better than you did, and get it quicker than you,' I snapped.

And then he shot back, 'So are you telling me I'm only in this band for my looks?'

I didn't respond but I never would have said to Lee that he was only in the band for his looks. I remember at the audition I thought Lee was the best-looking guy there, but once we were in the band together I just didn't see him like that at all. He maintains I said, 'You're only in this band for your looks.' While it wasn't particularly nice what I did say to him – that I was a better singer – at least I'd like to think it was the truth!

That was only the start of us arguing over tracks on that album. Lisa, Faye and Lee were keen we should write our own songs for that album, which I didn't think was a good idea for a band like us. Unless you have a Gary Barlow among you – someone who has a real gift for songwriting – it makes things more complicated. I guess they wanted the credibility of writing our own material, but whether it was good enough or not is another story. I, on the other hand, just wanted to sing. I didn't see songwriting as our strength

– we were a manufactured pop group and we were great at what we did and that was good enough for me.

To make it fair, we all ended up writing a song each. In the end I thought mine was all right for a first attempt at songwriting – I collaborated with Andrew Frampton who'd written a lot of our stuff, and it was called 'Hand On Your Heart'. It was actually about Reece, even though we hadn't been together for ages.

After the songs were written, everything became about splitting them up so we all got to sing a line here and a line there. They then started tracking up the songs a little bit (where it sounds like there's more than one person singing to give it a fuller sound) and, in some places, you couldn't actually tell who was singing what. I remember once having a disagreement with Lisa about who would sing a certain line live on stage because we couldn't actually work out who was singing it on the record! It certainly wasn't like the first two albums, where you could tell clearly who was singing the different parts. There are some good songs on *Buzz*, but I don't think it was our best album because of the way it was written and recorded.

It wasn't just my vocals that the rest of the band had a problem with. Tim and H were still together at this time, and everyone had started noticing that H had been getting more prominent vocals – particularly on 'Deeper Shade Of Blue' and 'When I Say Goodbye' from the *Steptacular* album – and I think it was felt that a bit of favouritism was going on. Faye was probably the most put out because it seemed like the parts that would have been hers before were being given to H.

Looking back, it seems to me that our management was often responsible for a lot of the whispers going on behind people's backs. You'd often hear from Tim what people were – or perhaps weren't – saying about you, which was unsettling and had the result of making tensions in the band worse. 'All the writers want to work with you, Claire,' he said to me when it came time to write our songs, 'because they think you're the best songwriter, so I'm putting you with Andrew.'

Of course it makes you think, 'Wow, they think I'm the best and I must keep that quiet from the rest of them.' But I remember being at the Brit Awards and hearing Tim say exactly the same thing to Lisa, EXACTLY the same thing!

It was one of the only times I've pulled someone up on something they'd done. Usually, I would have simmered on it, but I'd heard it with my own ears and I wanted him to know I'd caught him out, so I called him on it.

'Oh, you know, I had to say that to her,' Tim replied breezily. 'I have to make the others feel important.'

Tim always said to me all the way through, 'You're my Celine Dion' and 'When we do a solo record . . .' He always made me believe I was his favourite and I was the best, and that we just had to humour everyone else! For all I know, he was doing the same with everyone else in the band.

*

In the autumn we were planning for our 'Steps Into Christmas' arena tour, which kicked off in November. We had a few smaller warm-up shows beforehand and things didn't get off to a good start. We had this awful stylist who turned up at our first gig at Butlins in Minehead with rolls of fabric in the back of her van instead of costumes, so we had nothing to wear! We were all running around desperately trying to cobble together stage outfits because we were in the middle of nowhere and couldn't buy anything: it was a shambles. My mum and two aunties were sewing costumes together to help the stylist and the dressmaker!

For the arena shows in Sheffield I went shopping and bought the dancers loads of clothes, as well as my own outfits for the tour, while they were still making costumes in the corridor. It was like a panto! Even the set was like a panto – a big castle with steps coming down from it. It was awful!

On a more positive note, our next single 'Stomp' had been released and it rocketed into the charts, going straight to number one. *Buzz* was released soon afterwards and made it to number four in the album chart.

Although I was still thin at this point, I wasn't obsessing about my diet so much: Mark was a fitness freak so I had started going to the gym a bit more. If he was trying to shape up, all he'd eat was chicken with vegetables, so when we lived together that was pretty much all I cooked. He'd hardly ever let anything else pass his lips. Once I tried to put a Tic Tac in his mouth when he was driving and he chucked it out the window. He was a food Nazi! Occasionally we'd have a takeaway together, but it was once in a blue moon. I think he'd been scarred from a comment that was made about his weight early on in his career and it had stayed with him: when he first started dancing, one of his teachers said to him, 'If you want to make it in this business you have to lose weight.' He was obsessive about his body after that. I understood, though, after the comment Tim had made to me at the Steps audition.

Nor would it be long before my old diet demons returned with a vengeance.

After our 'Steps Into Christmas' tour, we all went our separate ways for the holidays. Then, at the start of 2001, we were booked to go to Japan for a couple of weeks on a promotional tour for *Buzz*, after which we planned to travel on to America to film a TV special for Nickelodeon.

Our single 'It's The Way You Make Me Feel' had been released on 1 January 2001 and made it to number two. I had far fewer vocals on that track than any of the others – I think I had two lines on the second bridge into the chorus. By now, we were all obsessed by how much we sang on any given track!

In Japan, I began to go back to my room and have dinner on my own every night. I didn't recognize anything on the menu apart from a burger and I thought, 'There's no way I can eat that.' So I ordered a tea plate of rice and a banana, and that's what I had for dinner every night for two weeks. During the day, I'd stick to a plain salad without dressing.

I'd been unhappy for a long time because of the way things had been going with the band and, once again, I was using my diet as a way of trying to regain some kind of control over my life.

When we got to LA, my body clock was all over the place – we'd gone from eight hours ahead of UK time to eight hours behind – and I kept waking up at 5 a.m. One morning, I went out and found a Starbucks, then walked for ages along an eerily deserted Sunset Boulevard. Everything was closed apart from a Virgin Megastore, so I went in and bought a Destiny's Child album, then went back to my hotel room and listened to it for the rest of the night.

The next day we had to do rehearsals for the Nickelodeon show; they'd set up a stage outside in a car park. When we broke for lunch they took us to a typical American burger joint, so I had no choice but to sit there and eat a burger with everyone else.

As soon as I'd finished it, I started panicking: I rushed back to where we were filming, found the toilets and stuck my fingers down my throat to try to make myself throw it up. All I could, think was 'I have to get this out. I can't get on stage with this inside me.' I'd been so strict with my diet in Japan and had eaten such plain food that I felt totally repulsed by the greasy burger I'd just swallowed.

I must have been in the toilet for ages because the burger just wouldn't come up. Eventually Lee came in and said,

'Are you all right, Claire?' I think he suspected what I was up to, but I just made out I didn't feel very well.

This wasn't the first time I made myself sick, but thankfully, it was never a regular occurrence because I'd become really good at just not eating. I knew I could control my weight that way, so I didn't have to make myself throw up.

As soon as I'd been sick I went back to work as if nothing had happened.

The rest of 2001 seemed to pass in a bit of a blur – our schedule was so rammed that all of us were exhausted and I just felt very low a lot of the time. I didn't feel like I fitted in or belonged with Steps any more. I didn't feel part of a team. And I really thought the rest of the band resented me for certain opportunities I'd been given and was convinced they were talking about me all the time.

I'd got a few little guest presenting opportunities by this time, including *CD:UK* with Ant and Dec and the BBC entertainment show *Electric Circus*, while H and I had presented a second series of *Steps To The Stars*.

The rest of the band weren't happy that H and I got to present the show in the first place, and when the second series was commissioned they were all saying, 'Can't someone else present it?' But the producers didn't want anyone else to host it, so we got to do it again. And a few little things like that kept happening.

I think the rest of the band felt we'd only got the *Steps*

To The Stars gig because the show's bosses liked us better or something, and not because we were any good at it. It was the same with the vocals – if I got to sing more on certain tracks it wasn't because I was a good singer; it was because the producers liked me better. This always bothered me. Not once did any of them ever say, 'You did a really good job on that, Claire,' or 'You sang that really well.' It was a very touchy subject.

But at least that year H and I gradually began to get closer again. We'd been such good mates originally and after our relationship had turned sour I had missed that friendship.

Mark and I started spending more time with H and Tim as a couple, and H started to travel to gigs and TV shows with me in the same car. Because we were spending a lot of time together, we started to open up to each other and it became apparent that he was unhappy with the way things were going in the band, too. I remember sitting in a dressing room with him before doing an episode of *Blue Peter* and we just started talking honestly about how we felt.

Neither of us wanted to be doing it any more, and we were both sick of compromising all the time. We were being given ultimatums about things having to change in terms of the vocals being shared out.

H and I had written a song called 'Stop Me From Loving You' that was going to be a B-side, so we went into the studio and recorded it. We didn't record anyone else doing lead vocals and the others weren't happy about that. But it was a B-side and, the way I see it, if you've written a song then you're not going to give the vocals to someone else, plus the key was really bloody high and best suited for our voices. What's more, Faye and Lisa had both recorded B-sides or album tracks on their own, and we had never complained about that.

One day, when the five of us were in a dressing room before a performance, Lee piped up that not one of us was a better singer than the other and that our voices were all just different.

'Lisa's got that nice, soft, pure kind of voice,' he said. 'But Claire, you can't do that. You've got the loud, powerful voice.'

I felt like saying, 'Have you not listened to any of our songs? Have you not heard "One For Sorrow", because that's pretty quiet.' Yes, I have got a loud voice: I can really belt it out, but that's not all there is to it, and it felt like I was being belittled or knocked down a peg or two to make sure I didn't get too big for my boots.

In May we released our next single – the double A-side 'Here And Now'/'You'll Be Sorry' and it rocked into the charts at number four. H sang quite a bit of the vocals on that one. During that spring we also recorded a few extra songs for the *Gold: Greatest Hits* album, which was due for release in October, then we were straight into rehearsals for the arena tour, which was kicking off in Sheffield in November.

Rumours were already circulating that Steps were splitting up. When any band puts out a greatest hits album people often assume it's the beginning of the end. We were asked on *SM:TV* if the rumours were true and we all denied it, although I was probably sitting there pondering my escape! But at that point I definitely didn't know for sure that I was going to leave, even though I felt like I didn't want to be doing it any more

Then, in July, something happened that put everything I was going through with Steps into perspective. One morning I was in the shower washing myself when I felt a strange lump in my left breast. I immediately panicked and assumed the worst – there can't be many scarier things for a woman than finding a breast lump. Oddly enough, the same thing had happened to my mum the year before and luckily the lump turned out to be benign, so I prayed that mine was nothing serious, too.

I knew how important it was to get it checked out as soon as possible, so I made an appointment straightaway. I didn't tell my mum, though – I didn't want to worry her after what she'd been through herself.

It was the first time I'd ever dealt with something with my partner instead of going straight to her. Mark was very calm and pragmatic. He kept reassuring me I'd be all right and that we just had to get it checked out and dealt with.

At the time, Steps was doing a lot of promotional interviews and performances, but I told management what had happened and that I'd booked an appointment to get it checked out because I was worried. I'll never forget the woman on our management team saying, 'But we've got radio interviews planned for that time. Can't you book it for another day?' I couldn't believe another woman was saying that to me after I'd just told her I'd found a breast lump. I was gobsmacked!

I still wasn't very good at speaking up for myself, but I really stood my ground. 'No,' I said. 'I'm going to the doctor. I've made the appointment as early as possible and I'll join you afterwards.' I never used to say anything in those interviews anyway – it was hard to get a word in edgeways with the rest of the band! And I knew no one would miss me as it wasn't like a TV interview, where it would have been obvious I wasn't there.

After I'd been for my initial appointment, the doctor then arranged for me to have a biopsy. I was really nervous about it and the night before I couldn't sleep as the possibility I might have cancer began to hit home. Luckily, I had the same doctor who'd treated my mum the year before and he put me at ease, and was really good at explaining what was happening.

It took an agonizing two weeks for the results to come back and it was a stressful wait, but Mark was very supportive. Thankfully, I was given the all-clear – the lump wasn't a cancerous tumour, but a benign fibroid cyst. The relief was immense.

When I told my parents after I'd been given the all-clear, Mum went mad and didn't speak to me for about a week –

I think it was just out of pure shock and worry. She'd been through an awful time with my granddad when he died of cancer and, after finding a lump herself, I think she was just extremely worried and angry that I hadn't confided in her.

It was a good thing I did decide to tell her, though, because some lovely person leaked the story to the papers and I ended up having to give interviews about my breast cancer scare – nothing was private any more.

We released our next single in September – a cover of the Diana Ross classic, 'Chain Reaction', and it leapt into the charts at number two. The vocals were quite evenly split on this song.

By the time the *Gold: Greatest Hits* tour got underway in November, relationships in the band had broken down so badly that we only saw each other when we got to the venue, and even then we'd eat dinner at different times with our own friends and family. And we barely talked to each other in the dressing room. When we went on stage we were always totally professional and gave the performance everything we had – the bad feeling between us never affected the job we did. But behind the scenes, we weren't interacting with each other at all unless we had to.

Sometimes during the day H, Mark and I would go shopping together, but most of my time was still spent with Mark, Shelina and the other dancers. That sheltered me to some extent but not entirely. For instance, one day, Tim told me that someone in the band was complaining that

Mark and I were swanning around like Posh and Becks, as if we owned the place! Apparently, they'd also said I'd been making myself sick to lose weight.

I know at that point I wasn't throwing up – I'd done it maybe a couple of times since LA, but when we got on tour I'd actually relaxed a little about my weight and was a bit bigger again. I had the usual insecurities about my bum and thighs, of course – we had these Moulin Rouge-type outfits and I had to get my legs out, which I panicked about, so I had some material hiding my backside. But I wasn't being sick at that point and I wasn't starving myself, either.

I don't know if it was just Tim stirring things up: maybe he wanted me to leave the group because H and I had become close again. If that was the case, I didn't realize at the time. If I'm honest, I've always had a tendency to be slightly paranoid – as I've said before, I really worry about what people think of me – so that kind of comment from Tim just fuelled it. I already assumed the others were talking about me behind my back. Now I actually thought they hated me.

I'd be in rehearsals – and this wasn't the case at all – but I felt that the others would deliberately be doing sit-ups and other exercises in front of me because I was eating something fattening that I shouldn't have been eating. My brain was saying, 'They're doing that to make you feel bad.' I honestly thought that they were trying to wind me up or make me feel shit about myself. Things had just got crazy.

*

One day in mid-December, when we were in Cardiff, Lisa came up to me in the dressing room and said, 'Do you think I'm jealous of you?'

'Uh, no, why?' I replied, thinking, 'Oh, shit, where is this going?'

'Well, that's what Mark told Lee last night at the wrap party,' she said. 'He told Lee I had a vendetta against you and that I was jealous of you. Do you think that's true?'

I was flabbergasted. Apart from anything else, Mark would never have said the word 'vendetta' because he's severely dyslexic and he simply wouldn't have used that word. In fact, when I confronted him about it later, he didn't even know what it meant!

Things were going nuts – it was like being at school again and this was just one example of how we were all behaving. Anyway, Mark was adamant he didn't say it, so I said, 'Right, well that's what Lee told Lisa, so you need to sort it out between you.'

Mark then spoke to Lee who apparently said, 'Yeah, I know you didn't, mate,' but when it came up in discussion later, it turned out that Lee was still telling everyone else that Mark *had* said it. To add to all of this, Lisa complained to Mark about his silver Gucci necklace because it was 'distracting' her on stage and demanded he took it off – even though he'd worn it throughout the entire tour and we only had a few shows left.

I remember just thinking, 'Arrrrgh! You know what, I'm

not doing this any more. I've had enough!' It was the point where I absolutely knew I had to leave the band.

I'd been mulling over leaving for a while, but now I knew for sure I couldn't work another day in that atmosphere. It sounds like a trivial argument to end the band over, but it really was the straw that broke the camel's back.

We'd just had a number-one album with *Gold: Greatest Hits* and our last single 'Words Are Not Enough'/'I Know Him So Well' had done well, too, making it to number five, and we were as popular with our fans as ever. I know a lot of people – including Faye, Lee and Lisa – think it was crazy that I decided to walk out when the band was at its pinnacle of success and popularity, but I didn't do it on a whim. I'd been unhappy for a very long time and I couldn't believe they hadn't realized that. But it was still an incredibly hard decision to make because I was walking out on everything I'd ever wanted.

In reality, though, the dream had turned sour. I just didn't feel comfortable in my own skin any more. I was passionate about singing and I wanted to be successful – I still do. But I couldn't cope with the other side of things at that time in my life – the band politics, the rivalry over vocals, the scrutiny that comes with being in the public eye. I'd been walking around for such a long time with a big knot in my stomach, and the only way I felt I could be rid of it was to walk away from Steps.

When I was young, my cousin had had a book about superstitions and it had said, 'If your initials spell a word, you're going to be rich and famous.' My initials spell CAR – Claire Anne Richards – so I was very excited by that, and used to dream about it coming true. But when I actually achieved it, I realized it wasn't all it was cracked up to be; that fame doesn't necessarily make you happy. Some people thrive on that kind of fame and attention, but I certainly didn't back then.

A lot of the time I was in Steps wasn't enjoyable for me and it should have been, and I do regret not making the most of all the opportunities that were handed to me on a plate. But hindsight is a wonderful thing, right? Maybe if I'd been less sensitive and had more of an 'I don't care' attitude, then I might have coped with things better, but I guess I'm just not built that way. You need a certain amount of ruthlessness to survive in this business and, back then, I wasn't tough enough. I worried far too much about what people would think of me and cared too much about upsetting other people. I'm sure I have upset people in my life and in my career, but it's usually because I've avoided a situation rather than dealt with it head-on.

I do think if we had discussed our problems then things might not have gone as far as they did. But I can't bear confrontation – I'd rather stew on something than cause a row, and I knew if I'd talked about what was upsetting me it would cause a problem, because discussing someone's talent is a delicate thing. It's just not something I would ever have done. I can be confident about my own abilities, but I certainly couldn't say to someone, 'Why should we share out the vocals when I'm a better singer than you?' That's what I would have needed to say, and I would have hated anyone to think I was being big-headed. At the end of the day, it wasn't my fault if I'd been given more lead vocals – I was being asked to sing those parts by our producers. And I was in the band to sing – if someone offered me vocals I was hardly going to turn round and give them away to someone else.

For me, being in Steps was only ever about the singing, and when that got overtaken by all of the other stuff, that's when it stopped being fun for me. I know I'm a good singer – that's the one thing I won't let anyone take away from me. The others used to say, 'We're all-rounders', and I was kind of offended, to be honest, because I'm not an all-rounder; I'm a singer. I don't want to be a dancer, I don't want to be an actress; all I ever wanted to do was sing. Given the chance, I would have stood still with a microphone, like the boys from Westlife.

After Lisa confronted me in Cardiff, I spoke to H. I was feeling quite calm, because I knew finally I was doing the right thing.

'I wanted to tell you that I've made my mind up,' I said. 'I'm leaving the band.'

'Well, I'm going, too,' he said simply.

After that, we spoke to Tim and he advised us to resign

before the end of the tour, rather than let the situation drag into the new year. Tim explained that because of our contracts we had to hand in resignation letters. He also told the record company about our decision.

Our last shows were at the MEN Arena in Manchester so, on 21 December, the day before our final show, it was decided we'd tell the rest of the band we were leaving. My mum, Auntie Chris and my sister Gemma drove up from London to be there for me because they knew how upset I'd be telling the others: I was a bit scared about how they would react and what they'd say to me, and I knew I'd feel intimidated.

We were having a meeting about four o'clock that day in the girls' dressing room to discuss filming the last show for Sky Box Office and for the live DVD, and for some reason it was me who got the job of telling everyone.

I started crying straightaway and I just blurted out, 'I can't do it any more. I have to leave and I won't be coming back in January. I just don't want this any more . . .'

I think everyone was shocked; which I find hard to believe, even now. I couldn't understand why they hadn't realized there was a problem and how miserable I was – at that point, we barely had a relationship with each other at all. I tried to explain everything as best I could, but I was crying a lot. Then H said, 'Yeah, and I'm leaving, too.' He handed over his resignation letter and walked out, leaving me to do the talking.

So much has been made of the fact that we handed over resignation letters there and then; we've been portrayed as cold and callous, but it wasn't like that at all. Legally we had to give them a resignation letter because we had a partnership agreement, but it was very basic, literally two sentences. But I *had* told them all first.

We also got stick for handing in our notice the day before the last show and a few hours before we had to go on stage and perform. But I had wanted to tell them to their faces, and I didn't want to do the final show of the tour knowing it would be our last ever while the rest of them were oblivious: I didn't think that was fair. I also knew that when I left they wouldn't be seeing me again and they'd just have got a phone call breaking the news, which I think would have been much worse.

Knowing the kind of person I am and what I'm like with confrontation, I think the fact that I sat there and told them to their faces was brave.

Afterwards I was relieved, but I was heartbroken, too. That last show on 22 December was one of the hardest things I've ever had to do in my life and I still don't know how I got through it. There's footage of the gig and, during the opening and closing sections, I'm just crying my eyes out because I knew that was the end.

I don't think Lee believed it would really happen – he probably just assumed I was having a strop. When we came offstage after that last show, the curtains closed and we all had a group hug. Lee wouldn't join in at first, but then he did.

'You'll be back, you'll be back in January,' he said just before he walked off.

I thought, 'No, I won't. I'm not coming back, I'm not . . .'

6

WITH HALF A HEART

That Christmas was one of the worst I've ever had. My dream lay in tatters and I was a complete mess. I'm sure Lee, Faye and Lisa assumed I was having a lovely time, but I wasn't. It was awful. One day my whole life was mapped out for me and being organized day-to-day by a management team, and the next I was thinking, 'What the hell do I do now? What's going to happen to me next?'

And, despite what the others may have thought, I was grieving for the band, too. I was relieved I'd found the courage to walk away but, nonetheless, Steps had been my entire life for the past five years and I felt incredibly sad that things turned out the way they did. The last person I saw that night in Manchester was Faye and we had a proper hug goodbye. We didn't even say anything to each other – we were crying our eyes out – but we both knew it was over and I'm glad we had that moment.

I went up to Leicester to spend the holidays with Mark

and his family. On Boxing Day, the story came out in the papers that Steps had split. We'd agreed to keep things quiet over Christmas and hold a press conference at the start of the new year, but the news was leaked before we had the chance. Our management had to quickly put out a statement from all of us, that started 'After five incredible years, we have decided it's time to move on to new challenges . . .' That didn't stop my phone ringing off the hook as friends, reporters and colleagues called to find out what had happened.

To make matters worse, the tabloids were all accusing us of conning our fans because so many of them would have gone out and bought Steps dolls and other band merchandise at Christmas: we were accused of cashing in, knowing we were about to split up. But that really wasn't the case: in our defence, it was only a couple of days before Christmas that H and I decided to hand in our notice – we hadn't been planning it for months beforehand.

But all of it put a real dampener on the festivities, to put it mildly. Not only had I lost my job, but it affected Mark, too, because dancing with Steps was a big part of his life as well. And I could tell that Mark's family thought I was being really rude by taking calls all the time. I don't think Mark's brother, Shaun, was very happy about all the phone calls and texting, but his wife Bhav, who's a dentist, was really supportive. Like me, she's from London but had made the decision to relocate to Leicester permanently with Shaun. She was so lovely to me and we'd sit and chat for hours. But it was a huge relief when Christmas was over and we could get back to London.

H and I had become really close again during that last year with Steps – we'd spent a lot of time with each other and we both liked the idea of working together in the future, but while we were still in the band we never discussed what that would actually be. Once the dust had settled following the Steps split, however, we began talking about what we could actually do.

In January 2002, Sony offered us a record deal. That ended up falling through, but at the last minute Warners came in with another offer and we signed to them to record as a pop duo called H & Claire. H was still with Tim at the time and he stayed on as our manager.

It did all happen really quickly after the band broke up, so I think Faye, Lisa and Lee all assumed we had known what we were doing before we handed in our notice, which wasn't the case. They've also said since that they found it odd because I said one of my reasons for leaving Steps was that I 'couldn't do it any more', but that then I went on to work with H. But the two of us were close at that point and it was quite a different situation. I never, ever wanted to give up singing; I just couldn't cope with being in Steps and all the politics that went along with it.

On 26 January, H and I appeared on the Saturday morning music show *CD:UK* with Cat Deeley, and announced our plans to start performing as H & Claire. It wasn't too long before we were being whisked off to Miami to shoot the video for our debut single 'DJ', either! It was great fun and probably the best video I'd ever done. We were in Miami for a whole week, even though it was only a two-day shoot, and we laughed the entire time we were there. I thought, 'This is amazing. I haven't felt like this for five years!' I felt truly happy and relaxed for the first time in a very long time.

Around the same time we were also offered a presenting gig on the Saturday morning kids' show *SM:TV*, which we'd appeared on a lot with Steps. We started working on that in April and had a brilliant time presenting alongside *Big Brother* 2 winner Brian Dowling and Tess Daly, who was a relative newcomer back then. The bit of the show I loved best was the comedy sketches we got to perform. When Ant and Dec had presented the show their sketch was called 'Chums' – a take on *Friends* – and ours was a *Big Brother* spoof called 'Big Bother'. I played a ditzy blonde, which apparently I was very good at!

They also made us do spoofs of songs, which was fine up until the week they asked me do Shakira. I was so embarrassed! I had to gyrate sexily to a comedy version of 'Whenever, Wherever' and I simply refused to do it in rehearsals. I just felt mortified. I knew I'd be able to do it fine when it came to the actual performance, but I've always found it really hard to switch on the stage-school smile when it's not for real. After that, I don't think the show's producers were particularly happy with me and I felt a bit of a change in their attitude towards me.

'DJ' was released in May and made it to number three in the singles chart where it spent a week in the Top 10. It was a promising start. And, that same month, Mark proposed to me.

I'd actually worked out he was going to do it because I'd found plane tickets to Rome just before leaving for Miami to shoot the video for 'DJ'. I'd filmed a video in Rome on the Spanish Steps when I was with the band and I'd told Mark what a beautiful and romantic location it was, so when I discovered those tickets I knew what he had up his sleeve.

While I was in Miami, the stylist we were working with had a stunning engagement ring and, a bit naughtily, I got her to call Mark and make up a story so he'd buy me a similar ring! I think she said something like, 'If you were ever going to propose to Claire, this is the ring she wants,' and then went on to describe it in great detail!

The day Mark proposed, I finished *SM:TV* at lunchtime and we headed off to the airport. All he'd told me was that we were flying to Italy.

Mark had booked dinner in the restaurant of a beautiful hotel, but we ended up missing it because the flight was delayed. When we finally got to Rome, we took a taxi to the Spanish Steps. It was about 10 p.m. and the place was packed with people. As soon as we stepped out of the car the heavens opened, and torrential rain started pounding the pavements.

At the time I put a good spin on the story when I was telling people. 'Then it started raining, so everyone left and we had the whole place to ourselves!' I'd say. In reality, I was trying to walk up the Spanish Steps balancing in Gucci heels, clutching an umbrella and trying really hard not to fall over and break my neck.

'Come on, Claire, let's look at the view,' Mark said enthusiastically as I tottered upwards.

All I could think was, 'You can't possibly be going to propose now, surely?!'

When we got to the middle section of the Steps, Mark got down on one knee . . . and I panicked. Even though I knew he was going to ask me, I told him to get up and I think I even told him to fuck off!

After I'd pulled myself together, I said yes, and then we walked back to the hotel in the rain. At the time I thought it was what I wanted, and I really did love him and was happy, but because I had known that Mark was going to propose, I didn't feel as much excitement as I should have done.

When we got to our hotel the restaurant was shut so we had toasted cheese sandwiches to celebrate! I wanted to call everyone back home and tell them my news, but they already knew. Mark hadn't been able to keep it to himself and he'd told all our friends and family he was going to ask me to marry him.

During my stint on *SM:TV* I noticed I'd started to put on a bit of weight, which began to worry me, not least because Tess, who I did the show with, was so tall, skinny and gorgeous. I'd probably only made a small leap from a size

8 to a size 10 to 12, but I'd noticeably filled out around my stomach and my clothes weren't fitting me so well.

I'm not sure what made me relax my diet – perhaps, initially, it was because I wasn't in the band with the girls any more and I wasn't constantly thinking, 'I look massive compared to Faye' or 'That outfit Lisa's wearing doesn't look like that on me.' Also, I wasn't as active as I had been in Steps because we weren't dancing as much, and I was eating at the ITV canteen a lot, which usually meant a plateful of stodge every day.

Just like I'd done with Faye and Lisa, I started to compare myself to Tess – luckily, I soon realized there was no point in even trying to look like her because I was never going to be that tall with long legs and a model-girl figure!

To try to nip the weight gain in the bud, I began seeing trainer Matt Roberts for the whole time I was on *SM:TV*. He had a gym in Jermyn Street, so I'd get picked up from rehearsals and go straight there. I exercised religiously, but I never actually lost much weight because I just kept eating crap, and I was eating at the wrong times, too.

My bad eating habits were a legacy from my days in Steps: grabbing junk on the run, not eating at regular intervals and quaffing loads of fizzy drinks. Because I discovered that Diet Coke gave me migraines it was a great excuse to stop drinking it and have regular Coke instead. I also skipped breakfast most of the time, then I'd be so ravenous I'd stuff down a calorie-packed muffin mid-morning. I was probably going out a bit more at that point, too, so I was drinking more alcohol.

I was papped a few times with a little tummy, which got the 'circle of shame' treatment in *Heat* magazine. I was a bit spotty at the time, too, which also got picked up on, so I went to see a dermatologist and got a prescription for Roaccutane. I'd had this problem before in the early days of Steps when I was just coming out of my teens – I remember sitting in the Prev one night going to our next gig and crying my eyes out while the others were sleeping because my spots were hurting so much. I didn't want my skin to get that bad again and I definitely didn't want to be a spotty bride, so I took a four-month course.

At home, however, I wasn't eating any more healthily than I was when I was at work. I was on my own quite a lot of the time because Mark used to go off on tours as a backing dancer with bands like Blue. So, instead of cooking healthy homemade meals or Mark's favourite chicken and veg dinner, I was just having takeaways all the time: Indian, Chinese, pizza. You name it; I ordered it.

I'd also bought some slimming tablets in America and decided to take them in a fit of desperation to see if they made any difference. They had ephedrine in them, which boosts your metabolic rate, helps burn fat and suppresses appetite. But because it's a stimulant, it also makes your heart race and gives you tons of extra energy. Because I'd never taken drugs, I didn't really have a clue what I was doing at the time or what to expect from a stimulant. I didn't take the full dose because I was a bit scared, but one night when Mark was away I was still awake at 5 a.m. baking batches and batches of cakes: cheesecakes, fairy cakes, cookies. It was like a production line in my kitchen. Who does that when they're taking slimming pills?

Bhav had bought me a Nigella Lawson cookbook and because I'd always loved baking and hadn't done it for such a long time, I suddenly thought, 'Right, I'm going to go through this entire book and bake everything in it.' I just didn't feel tired, and wanted to make good use of all this 'energy' I had.

Eventually I ran out of ingredients and the only twenty-four-hour supermarket I could think of was the Tesco on Brompton Road. I drove all the way there to get more ingredients at three o'clock in the morning, before coming back and carrying on with more baking. I was literally off my head on slimming pills!

I didn't actually eat any of the stuff I made as, once I'd baked everything, I froze it all, including rolls and rolls of cookie dough, so I could slice bits off when I needed it and stick it in the oven. In fact, I ended up throwing it all out a couple of months later.

I stuck with the slimming pills for a while, but I never seemed to lose any weight. When they ran out I tried to get some more, but the ones sold here didn't have the ephedrine in them, so luckily that put an end to any more slimming aids.

*

One day in July I was at the studio in rehearsals for *SM:TV* when my mobile rang. I grabbed it out of my bag and saw it was Gemma calling.

'Hi, Gemma, what's up?' I answered breezily.

'Er, I thought I'd better call to let you know that Mum's left Dad,' she replied.

'What?' I asked, frantically trying to take in this bombshell.

'Yeah, she left without saying anything because she didn't want any fuss.'

As Gemma's words began to sink in my eyes filled with tears, and I could feel my heart aching. My parents had been together for thirty years.

I know people think when you're an adult you should be able to cope better if your parents break up, but it was such a massive shock and I couldn't come to terms with it. I even remember wishing that they'd split up when I was a kid, so I could have had years to get used to the idea.

I'd had twenty-four years of happy Christmases, birthdays and holidays and I couldn't imagine how things were going to work in our family any more, or how we'd cope with the changes. When Gemma and I were growing up, our house was always the house in the neighbourhood where all our friends would come after school and at weekends, and they'd all help themselves to food from the fridge. Our mum and dad were the parents everyone liked. I never, ever thought they'd split up – and remain separated. It wasn't an amicable split either – it was horrible.

At first I thought it was my fault because my mum used to love coming along to Steps gigs with my Auntie Chris, but all that had gone when the band split up. It meant she was spending a lot more time at home with my dad and, if they weren't happy, I thought maybe that had made things worse. Our family dynamics had changed, too – Mum's whole life had been about me and my sister, but we'd grown up and weren't around as much.

My parents have always been very different people – my dad is non-confrontational and would rather ignore problems than risk an argument, whereas Mum wants to discuss things and sort them out. They'd also got together very young, and I guess they just grew apart over the years.

Mum had said she wanted to leave Dad a few months before, but we had managed to persuade her not to. But when she turned fifty that July, she left; and there was no going back. She'd rented a flat for herself and walked out without telling anyone where she was going, and she wouldn't speak to us for a little while. I guess she just needed some space to come to terms with what was happening. Gemma was still living at home with Dad, so she was on the spot to support him and help take care of practical things like cooking and laundry.

Things were pretty horrible, though. Everything Gemma and I had grown up with had changed in the blink of an eye, and I couldn't help wondering if any of those lovely childhood memories had been real. I always thought we were happy and I thought my parents were happy too. It was just so upsetting for all of us.

I was having doubts about my career as well. In August, H and I released our second single 'Half A Heart'. It peaked at number eight, which wasn't too bad, but at the back of my mind, I was wondering if, when I left Steps, I should have gone solo and done a big ballad album. I wasn't brave enough to do it then; I worried about the timing being wrong and that it would have been rushed. Jo O'Meara tried to do that after S Club 7 and it didn't work, so I'm not sure it would have worked for me at that point either – everyone still wanted Steps. It's very difficult to get it right: Robbie Williams managed it, but only after a few singles and if he hadn't had 'Angels', he might not have made it either.

I don't like failing at anything and I'd rather not do something if I think I might fail, which has probably held me back a hell of a lot in my life, as I tend to pre-empt everything by imagining what might go wrong. Sticking with H seemed safe and it was the easy option, but we probably rushed into it.

I remember being on a photo shoot one day and someone on the team snapped at me over something. I ended up locking myself in the toilet for about an hour and a half, crying my eyes out, all over something really stupid. We had a packed itinerary as usual and I just kind of broke, I suppose. Jackie had to take me home because I was in such a mess.

I was just completely worn out. We'd gone straight from Steps into the H & Claire thing and presenting *SM:TV* and, on top of that, we'd been doing gigs all summer and were now starting to promote our next single and album. I hadn't really taken a moment to sit back, take a breath and consider things properly.

We released our third single on 2 November – a double A-side with 'All Out Of Love' and a cover of Disney's 'Beauty And The Beast', which made it to number ten and stayed there for about three weeks. I hadn't wanted to put out 'All Out Of Love' because it sounded too much like Steps. Our first single had been quite disco-dancy, but the second one was a little bit cooler and I wanted to go more down that road. But because the second single hadn't done as well, the management panicked and went for a track they thought was a safer option and would have more commercial success.

Management had also been trying to force us to record 'You're The One That I Want' as our next single, which I really didn't want to do. The idea of H and me morphing into Olivia Newton John and John Travolta and singing that song to each other just seemed totally ridiculous!

When our album *Another You, Another Me* was released, on 18 November, it peaked at number fifty-eight in the album chart. And, not long after that, I refused to do anything else.

All of these things were building up and I felt like I was on the verge of a breakdown. I was worried about how our first family Christmas would be since Mum and Dad had split up and everything had got on top of me all of a sudden: it felt like things were spiralling out of my control again. I didn't want to put a brave face on it any more and I also couldn't stand the embarrassment of turning up at TV and radio shows to promote the album, when everyone knew it hadn't been the success it should have been. I kept having visions of Lisa, Lee and Faye getting together to have a good old laugh at me and H!

We had a few promotional things leading up to Christmas and it got to the point where, after agreeing to another appearance, I rang one of our managers, Vicky, and said, 'I'm not doing anything else after that. I can't face it.'

H and I had a pre-existing commitment to perform at Disneyland Paris in January 2003 because we'd recorded the song for the re-release of *Beauty And The Beast*. It was the last thing we did as H & Claire – and it was a shambles! They were holding a big Princess Ball to celebrate the ten-year anniversary of the film, during which we would sing our cover version of 'Beauty And The Beast'. We'd done a rehearsal in the afternoon so we knew the plan was for us to start singing, and then all the Disney characters would walk out from the back of the stage to join us.

We weren't singing live for some reason and, that evening, when we were waiting in the wings to perform for real, the song suddenly started playing before we could get on stage and pick up our mics. H and I were frozen to the spot.

'Isn't that your song? Get on the stage!' someone shouted.

Then the characters started parading on and I thought, 'There's no way I'm walking out there when my voice is already blaring out of the speakers, then picking up my mic!' It was too late to stop the characters coming down, so the Beast, Belle, Prince Charming and Cinderella all came on stage then stood there looking confused in front of two empty mic stands. After a second, they did all their waving, and shuffled off again.

The show's director wanted us to go back on and perform the song again, but refused to send the characters back down. It was all very funny and chaotic.

H and I had had a laugh that year and we made a lot of money, but it wasn't working for us and we both accepted we would call it a day. After that, I just kind of shut down. I felt like I had to get away from it all for a while. The *SM:TV* job had also come to an end when we released the album, so I put all thoughts of work and singing to the back of my mind and, for the next eight months, channelled all my energy into planning my wedding to Mark.

I'd started to comfort eat a little bit at this point – I was upset and worried about my parents, my career had imploded and I had a lot more time on my hands. And the more upset I got about things, the more I ate and the less I went out – it was a cycle that would continue during my marriage to Mark. I'd stay in bed till midday because I had nothing to do, then I'd watch telly all day unless I had to see a florist or look at a wedding venue.

One day Melanie, who worked at the Odeon cinema, rang and said that their freezers had broken down so she had to get rid of tons of Häagen-Dazs ice cream. She asked if I wanted some and, being a lover of ice cream, I thought,

'Yeah, all right.' I was expecting it to be little pots, but I ended up with industrial-size tubs of Cookies & Cream in my freezer. I managed to get through the lot.

I was on the slippery slope to overeating.

Our wedding was booked for 1 August 2003, a couple of weeks before my twenty-sixth birthday. Like lots of little girls, I grew up imagining exactly how my wedding would be. I wanted to arrive in a horse-drawn carriage like Princess Di and wear a dress like the one Kim Basinger wore in the movie *My Stepmother Is An Alien*, which had a cut-out heart at the back. As it was, the wedding was fabulous but, if I'm completely honest, I think I was more in love with the idea of a wedding than I was with Mark.

Before I got married, I had had flashes of doubt that Mark wasn't the one for me, but it felt like things had gone too far to put a stop to it. We argued so much about the seating arrangements and who'd been invited and who hadn't, but because everyone tells you it's normal to have rows when you're organizing a wedding, I just carried on with it, hoping I'd feel differently afterwards. On my wedding day, I even remember thinking, 'I wonder if Reece will turn up and try to stop the wedding like Dustin Hoffman in *The Graduate*,' but of course he didn't. Although he did say later that if he'd known where the wedding was, he would have!

On the run up to the wedding it rained non-stop every single day for about a fortnight, then on the day itself the sun came out from behind the clouds and it was the hottest

Left H and I had become close again during the final year of Steps, so we jumped at the chance to record as H & Claire.

Above With Shelina at our friend Solomon's wedding, in my favourite Matthew Williamson dress.

Look how happy I am to be back with Reece in 2005.

Left I really enjoyed *Celebrity Masterchef*, but I was horrified by how fat I looked. Soon after, I jumped at the chance to lose weight and do a fitness DVD.

Below I immediately fell in love with my beautiful son Charlie, born on 8 May 2007.

Right Gemma was my bridesmaid when I married Reece on 1 November 2008. I'd slimmed down for the wedding and felt wonderful.

Below right The whole day was lovely – I wish we could do it again!

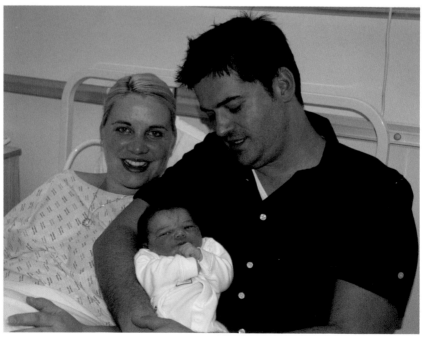

Above and left On our honeymoon in Thailand.

Above right Daisy was born on 29 December 2009. She is so gorgeous.

Right Being a mum to Charlie and Daisy is what keeps me grounded.

Far right In June 2010 I was dieting again to lose the weight I'd put on when pregnant, but this time I was determined to take it more slowly.

Left I loved my time on *Popstar to Operastar*. Not only did I get to wear gorgeous gowns but I regained my confidence as a singer.

Right and below right On holiday in Tenerife in 2011.

Left I now know I can be
happy as a size 12, 14 or
even a 16 and a tight dress
will showcase my curves!
On ITV1's *Lorraine*,
presenting the show's
Cake Club in 2012.

Below Reunited with
Steps and performing live
on *This Morning* in October
2011. I was terrified, but
the joyful energy in the
studio reminded me of
what Steps had meant
for the fans.

day of the year. The setting was stunning – the venue was a fairy-tale castle with a little church in Northamptonshire called Castle Ashby. It really was absolutely beautiful.

I spent a fortune on creating my perfect day and I paid for the whole thing myself – we decided not to do a deal with a celebrity magazine as I wanted the wedding to remain private and I didn't want it being constantly interrupted by photo sessions.

My mum and dad bought me a beautiful Vera Wang wedding dress and I had a bouquet of real calla lilies – I'd never forgotten the fake ones I'd carried when I played the part of Maria in *The Sound Of Music* at secondary school all those years before!

The castle had a courtyard in the middle where we'd put Moroccan tents with bars, and there was an enormous marquee built off the side of the castle. We'd invited more than 200 people for the wedding breakfast at £150 a head; all in all, I must have spent over £100,000 for the wedding of my dreams. Looking back now it seems ridiculous to have spent that much money, but I guess I had it at the time.

One of my problems is that I do like to spend money! Throughout my time with Steps I spent a lot of it. I bought a £30,000 Mercedes sports car when I was twenty and I remember my mum saying, 'You're mental!' but my dad was really excited about it. When I went to my bank to get the cheque to pay for it, the woman behind the counter said, 'Is it the deposit for a house?' and I had to say, 'No, it's for a car!' I also bought my mum designer handbags, my dad a Cartier watch for Christmas and my sister a car.

H and I used to go into Dolce & Gabbana all the time – it was our favourite shop. Once we popped in before doing a TV show when H & Claire was still going and, when we got back to the BBC, H said, 'How much did you spend in there?' and I said 'I don't know.' I really didn't have a clue: I hadn't even looked at the receipt. I'd spent nearly £2,000 in twenty minutes. I only ever had a debit card because the money was in the bank so I'd just hand it over without even looking at the price tag.

I remember, too, that I got invited to appear on the BBC2 music show *Never Mind the Buzzcocks* and I had in my head what I wanted to wear – a black Dolce & Gabbana shirt with a diamond cross. I think I'd seen someone with that look and I wanted to copy it, so I took myself off to the jeweller, Asprey, on Bond Street and bought myself a diamond cross just to go on that show. Stupid! I suppose I just thought the money was always going to be there.

I had the same extravagant attitude to the wedding. Mark didn't really pay for any of it so I felt I could go a bit crazy and have what I wanted. Afterwards, though, whenever we had an argument, he'd throw it back in my face and say, 'Well, I didn't want all that anyway.' But he still invited the world and his wife – some of the guests were people I'd only said hello to once!

All of my friends and family were at the wedding – Dad gave me away and Gemma and Shelina were bridesmaids.

I felt so nervous walking down the aisle and a little bit freaked out that all eyes were on me to see what I looked like. During the vows it got to the bit where I had to say '. . . and all that I have I share with you' and I turned to the congregation and made a funny face. It didn't go down well with Mark's brother, but everyone else laughed!

There weren't many celebrities there – there was H, the boys from Blue, Brian Dowling; and Shaznay Lewis from All Saints also came because Mark was good friends with her boyfriend, Christian Storm.

I'd asked Cossie from TSD to sing because we'd remained close over the years and I thought of her as a loyal friend: her house got burgled once when I was still in Steps and I sent her money on a bike straightaway so she could replace all her stuff. But, just before the wedding, she called to say she'd got a gig in Newcastle and that she couldn't sing at the wedding, but could still make it to the reception. I felt really hurt and just said, 'You know what, Cossie, don't bother.' If I'd asked her to be a bridesmaid, would she have done the same thing? But, looking back, I feel really bad about that because we were so close. If Cossie hadn't left TSD, then I might never have sent out tapes for auditions and got into Steps. It was easy for me to have those standards, I guess, because I'd made it and didn't feel like I couldn't turn down a gig. But it's hard for things to be the same when a good friend goes back on a promise, and it wasn't the first time she'd let me down.

Although the wedding was absolutely beautiful and I'm

sure all the guests had a fantastic time, I didn't enjoy myself at all. I hadn't slept properly the night before because I'd kept going over all the arrangements in my head to make sure I'd done everything. I was knackered, and kept taking myself off to a quiet room to sit by myself. After months of planning, I just felt a bit disconnected from it all.

When the dinner and speeches were over we had our first dance and, after that, I didn't see Mark again until we went to bed at 5 a.m. – he was off drinking and dancing with his mates. I never went back to the dance floor.

The following day, things only got worse and Mark and I ended up having a bit of a row in front of everyone over what we were going to do with a massive bunch of white roses he'd bought me.

His brother had got married before us and the centre-piece from their top table had been laid where their granddad's ashes were scattered. We'd agreed to do something similar, but there were one hundred roses in the bouquet that Mark had given me so, because we were going on honeymoon, my idea was to split it up and give some to my mum, some to his mum and his nan, then place the rest where his granddad's ashes were scattered. We ended up having an argument because Mark wanted to put the whole bunch of roses by a bench in the cemetery.

'They're my flowers; I should be able to do what I want with them,' I said to him at one point.

Apparently I really upset his brother and I know that after that I was labelled as being selfish, but I just thought it was wasteful: I wanted to let other people enjoy the flowers, too. In my opinion we didn't need to put all one hundred roses on the ground – they weren't even going to be placed on a grave. So that was our first argument as husband and wife.

After spending all that money on the wedding, I spent another £30,000 on our honeymoon. We went to America for a month and it was an amazing holiday, although pretty exhausting because we did a lot of travelling. We flew to New York and stayed there for a few days; then we flew on to San Francisco. The idea was to hire a car and drive down to LA, but when we went to pick up the car, Mark realized he'd forgotten to bring his driver's licence. We'd agreed I wasn't going to drive in the US because I'd never driven on the other side of the road before and was nervous, so our only option was to get on a Greyhound bus!

During our honeymoon, I found out that the photographer who shot our wedding was planning to provide photos of it to *Now* magazine. She was a friend of Tim's, who was still my manager, and when she'd asked originally I remember saying very firmly, 'No, I don't want to sell the photos. If anything, let's just give the press one shot if they're bothered, and there's no point in asking for money for that.'

Tim called when we were in San Francisco and said, 'The magazine will be out next week and the photos are on the H & Claire website.'

I couldn't believe what I was hearing. I hadn't given permission for the photos to be put on the website, for one thing. And Tim said that the photographer had told him that I'd said it was OK for the pictures to appear in *Now* magazine and that she could keep the money, which was certainly not what I'd said. Even if there had been some sort of misundertsanding by the photographer, I felt Tim should have realized that it didn't make sense – if I was going to let a magazine have exclusive photographs of my wedding, I would have sold them myself to *OK!* Magazine and had my wedding paid for into the bargain!

I started freaking out because it really felt to me like I'd been stitched up and I got lawyers involved to try to stop the magazine printing the pictures. But I spent loads of time on stressful phone calls and £10,000 in legal bills for nothing.

So, that ruined the first few days of our honeymoon; then I had to sit on a Greyhound bus for hours instead of driving down the Pacific Coast Highway in an amazing convertible sports car with the wind in my hair! My dad found Mark's licence and shipped it to America, but it ended up chasing us round the country for ages, just missing us at every stop.

We stopped off at an amazing hotel called the Post Ranch Inn in Big Sur near Carmel with the most beautiful views over the Pacific Ocean – sadly we only stayed one night because it was so expensive. Then we got a cab to take us further down the coast to Santa Barbara and we stopped at the Madonna Inn on the way. Eventually the licence arrived when we got to the Four Seasons in Santa Barbara, and from there we drove to Laguna Beach and on to San Diego.

Pretty much as soon as we arrived in San Diego, however, we started arguing because we got lost, and then we got to our hotel and it was a bit rubbish after all the lovely hotels we'd stayed in, so we ended up moving somewhere else. From San Diego we flew to Las Vegas for a few nights, then on to Los Cabos in Mexico for ten days.

We were sitting by the pool at our gorgeous hotel, Las Ventanas, when I spotted Simon Cowell, who was there with his then girlfriend Terri Seymour and his brother, who was writing his autobiography. I'd met Simon before when I was in Steps and Mark had worked with Terri when she was a model and dancer. Terri came over to chat to us, then Simon and his brother walked over to say they were going to lunch. Terri introduced us and said to Simon, 'Do you know Claire?'

'Claire from . . .?', he replied, looking confused. Maybe I'd put on a bit of weight during my month in America and OK, I had no make-up on, but I still looked like myself! Didn't I?

I was just thinking should I say, 'Claire from Steps', which I would have found really embarrassing, when he seemed to catch on.

'Oh, yeah, you look great, you look amazing!' Simon said, and was incredibly gushy. But I just remember wondering, 'Was that a showbiz snub?'

The day before we were due to leave, Jennifer Aniston and Courteney Cox arrived at the hotel, which was very exciting because I was the biggest *Friends* fan when I was younger. We were in the gym one day – Mark was still obsessed with keeping in shape, but I just used to walk on the treadmill for an hour while watching telly – when they walked in. I stayed on the bike for an extra hour so I could exercise next to Courteney, who was on the cross trainer reading a script. Both she and Jennifer were tiny and beautiful.

I kept punching Mark because I was so excited, but he wasn't really that bothered. If we'd been at the hotel longer I might have tried to make friends with them – or just stalk them!

Almost as soon as we got back from our honeymoon Mark had to go on tour with Blue. The day he left I drove him to the tour bus and I gave him an iPod I'd bought for the trip, which I'd loaded up with music. We hugged goodbye before he jumped on board and the bus roared off.

I was on my own again. When I got home to an empty house that day, I headed straight for the fridge to raid it for leftovers or treats.

On the lead-up to the wedding I'd bought a running machine so I could lose a few pounds before the big day, but I just didn't commit to it or to an eating plan, so I didn't actually lose any weight for the wedding. My dress was a size 12, although it had to be taken in a bit, so I wasn't big at all, just bigger than I had been in Steps. After the wedding was over, though, I gradually began putting on more weight and I crept up to a size 14.

Mark had started to say things to me like, 'You need to

lose weight' or 'You need to go to the gym.' If we'd got ready to go out and I was all done up, I'd say, 'Do I look all right?' and he'd reply, 'Well, yeah, you look all right, but you'd look better if you lost a few pounds' or 'You'd look better if you were a size smaller.'

I feel bad saying that Mark criticized me over my weight – I don't actually think he was being nasty, I just think it was the way he was. He was this super-fit dancer and I didn't fit his ideal, and it was just another reason why we weren't right for each other. I don't think he really loved me for who I was – he fell in love with 'Claire Richards, the skinny blonde pop star' and when I wasn't that any more, he didn't really like it.

He was probably trying to help by saying those things, but they didn't help and, in fact, they only made me want to do the opposite and stuff my face. I used to eat when I was out shopping and pretend I hadn't, or I'd buy two cakes and hide one in the cupboard. I started snacking with my head hidden by the open fridge or cupboard door so he couldn't see what I was doing – hiding food from him just became a habit, and I used to love it if he went out as it meant I could get myself a takeaway.

Whenever he was away on tour I never really went out. If people invited me somewhere I'd either make an excuse straightaway about why I couldn't go, or I'd agree to go, then at the last minute I'd let them down. I dreaded the thought of going out and the stress of trying to find an outfit that would make me feel slimmer.

I didn't go to red-carpet events any more, either. By this time I'd started talking to the other members of Steps again and I remember going to see Faye in a theatre production in the West End. There were photographers outside and I didn't think anything of it, but the next day there were huge pictures of me splashed all over the *Sun*, standing next to Faye, alongside stories commenting on my weight gain. That was the first time people started noticing that I was bigger.

By this point I think I was actually depressed. I'd started to feel really crap about myself and, on the rare occasions I did go out for the night with Mark, I'd start crying because none of my clothes would fit me. Sometimes I felt so upset I'd be unable to leave the house. I just got deeper and deeper into this pit of depression and then I just stopped going out altogether – I didn't want to go anywhere.

I didn't even know how to cook sensible meals: I'd cook a huge amount of food that was enough for a family, then I'd just split it in two and eat my half. That's where my overeating really started: I had a distorted idea of portion sizes and I just didn't know when to stop eating. I'd always clear my plate no matter how much food was piled on it, just like I'd done when I was a little girl.

Eventually, I knew it wasn't right that I was feeling so down, so I decided to see my doctor about it. I sat in the surgery crying my eyes out because I didn't really know what to do with myself. My entire life since leaving school had revolved around being in a pop group. I felt absolutely hopeless.

I knew I still wanted to sing but I've never been the kind of person who can pick up the phone and say, 'Do you want to manage me?' as I was always too scared people would say, 'Sorry, who are you?' and I'd have to explain what I'd done. I never really thought anyone would be that interested or bothered about me any more.

The doctor prescribed antidepressants and I took the first course, but I didn't really want to accept that I was depressed. I think I felt it was an excuse for not being happy with Mark. Plus I'd had friends who'd taken antidepressants for years and I didn't want to get into that cycle of dependency. So I stopped taking the antidepressants after the first lot was finished, but I can't say I pulled myself out of my black mood. It would take me years to feel properly content and happy.

I would have felt stupid going back to see my doctor after I'd stopped taking the pills, so I didn't – I was convinced she'd think everything I was saying was silly and trivial. I expected her to say, 'Come and meet someone who's got real problems.' Apparently that's what lots of people with depression think, and it stops them getting the help they need.

Things got worse when, towards the end of 2003, Auntie Pauline, my mum's sister, got ill, which was a huge blow for all of us in the family. Growing up, my mum's sisters were a big part of our lives. Dad's brother John had emigrated to Australia and his sister Anne lived in America, so it was Mum's family that was always around. Auntie Pauline loved Steps as much as my other aunties and would always come to see us at Wembley.

She'd been feeling unwell for a while and had a cold she couldn't shift, so she went to the doctor and was told she had pneumonia. Then, in the new year, she was diagnosed with lung cancer and given just three months to live.

I immediately thought, 'That's not true, she'll be fine. There's no way she's going to die.' I suppose that's my way – if I don't want something to happen, I just stick my head in the sand and convince myself it's going to go away. I was in denial.

She was tall and slender and seemed quite a tough lady on the outside. And she was always busy with something – zooming around from one place to the next, smoking like a chimney. Whenever she turned up on the doorstep she'd always say, 'I'm not stopping; I'm just having a quick coffee.' I used to joke that she ought to have the words 'I'm not stopping!' on her gravestone.

If you were ever ill or if there was a crisis, Auntie Pauline was always the first one there to offer a helping hand or a shoulder to cry on. My mum said even if they'd fallen out about something, she'd still turn up if she needed her. And she was always having lonely old ladies round for a home-cooked dinner – she was a kind person.

That Christmas, Auntie Pauline had come to me and asked if I could lend her some money because they needed something for the cab firm she ran with her husband, Carl.

She asked me for £20,000. It was, literally, all I had at the time, because most of the money I'd earned with Steps and H & Claire had long gone, especially after my lavish wedding to Mark.

I was a little bit scared of Auntie Pauline to be honest, so I didn't feel I could say no, and I gave her all my savings.

I remember when she was first diagnosed she was very sick and the whole family went to see her in hospital. My mum is from a big family and we're a close-knit bunch – we might not see each other for a while and we fall out sometimes but, when it matters, we're there for each other. My dad was also at the hospital, to support us all, even though he and my mum were separated.

I sat in the waiting room for ages because I was worried about how I'd react to seeing Auntie Pauline so ill and I didn't want to upset her. For some reason, everyone has always thought that I'm the one in the family who needs most protection if anything bad happens. I'm too sensitive, I suppose. So my mum and dad took hold of my arms and walked me along the corridor to her room. As soon as she saw me she started crying and I gave her a hug. No one knew I'd given her any money, so I leaned in close and whispered in her ear, 'Fucking hell, this is a bit of a drastic way to get out of paying me that money back.'

She started laughing. 'Wicked cow!' she whispered back.

After that I just convinced myself Auntie Pauline was going to get better. When she was discharged from hospital,

Gemma, Michelle, her daughter, and I took her for lunch somewhere new every week.

I'm a big believer that everything happens for a reason and, because I wasn't working, I was able to spend more time with my family than I had in a long time. If I'd still been with Steps I would never have got that precious time with my auntie.

If I needed confirmation that all was not well with my marriage, I got it on our first wedding anniversary in August 2004. Mark's friend Christian Storm had arranged his stag weekend in Spain on the same date, and I couldn't believe it when Mark said he was going. When I challenged him over it he just became very defensive and tried to make out I was the one who was out of order. But even though things weren't going great with us, it was important to me that we spent our anniversary together.

Eventually, Mark altered his plans so we could spend the weekend with each other, but I took him to the airport on the Sunday night, which was our actual anniversary, so he could fly out to Spain for the rest of the stag do. It just seemed that Mark was constantly putting everyone else in front of me – even on our wedding anniversary.

While he was away with his mates, a friend of ours called Solomon, who was business partners with my first agent Paul Fitzgerald, was getting married in Rhyl. I'd known Solomon since I was a teenager, so I was keen to go – H and I had missed Paul's wedding because we were doing H & Claire at the time and had also known that Lee, Faye and Lisa would be there and we didn't want to cause trouble. But I really didn't want to miss Solomon's wedding, so I went by myself – and got very drunk! I was wearing my favourite frock – a short pink empire-line Matthew Williamson dress with shoestring straps. It was probably the last time I was able to go bra-less because of the weight I'd been putting on.

Shelina was there with her husband; Faye was there with Jasper; and Dane Bowers was also there. Another Level had split up in 2000 and Dane was now a DJ and record producer who'd worked with True Steppers and Victoria Beckham. Years before he'd told Lee that he fancied me, but nothing came of it because he was dating Katie Price.

At the end of the night I got a cab back to the hotel with Dane and another guest, and we both said goodnight and went our separate ways. When I got back to my room I wasn't ready for the night to end, so I decided to knock on Dane's door and ask him if he could help me undo my dress! I fancied him a bit and I was up for a flirt.

We chatted for ages about what was going on in our lives, then he started kissing me and we ended up having a bit of a fumble, although we didn't have sex. However, I did wake up in his bed fully clothed the next morning and had to do the walk of shame. I didn't want to leave his room wearing the same outfit I'd worn to the wedding because I knew that would look bad, so I wrapped a big towel around me, tucking my dress straps underneath to hide them, so it looked like I'd just popped into his room to borrow something.

I gave Dane a lift back to London that day and, as I dropped him off, I said to him, 'I'm married; I can't do this.'

'I think that's a real shame,' he replied. 'We could have given it a go.'

When I got home, Mark was back from the stag do and I put what happened with Dane to the back of my mind. I don't remember feeling bad about it, though. I'd gone out of my way to create the situation and I clearly wanted something to happen between me and Dane. It was the only time I ever did anything like that – maybe it was because he reminded me a lot of Reece to look at.

I might not have slept with Dane, but I was someone else to add to his long list of liaisons!

I don't think Mark and I were ever really sexually compatible. I never felt the same passion I'd felt for Reece at the beginning, but I convinced myself the only reason it was so good with Reece was because we were having an affair. I began thinking a normal relationship was more like the one I had with Mark, and that my not wanting sex much wasn't unusual.

Deep down, I'd never lost the feelings I had for Reece – I just tried to suppress them. When I was still with H & Claire I'd occasionally drive to where he was working just to catch a glimpse of him – he'd left the music business by then and owned a posh gift shop in Teddington High Street, but I never wanted to talk to him. During those years we were apart, every now and then we'd send each other a text to say hi. When we first broke up we'd had those text rows, but as the years went on we'd send each other a 'Merry Christmas' or a 'Happy birthday' or just a 'How are you?' We stayed connected, even though we didn't speak to each other.

I should never have married Mark. It was unfair. I'd met him on the rebound from Reece and I'd never gone out and sowed my wild oats. Mark was in the right place at the right time, but we had very little in common and, once the H & Claire thing stopped, that became glaringly obvious. The reason we had worked as a couple was because we were working together and we talked about our jobs and we had the same friends. But when I stopped working we lost that connection. It sounds like a cliché, but while I loved Mark, I was never in love with him like I had been with Reece.

By the autumn, Auntie Pauline had deteriorated a lot. One day she asked Gemma to cut her hair really short before her treatment made it fall out, and we both gave her a wash. I'll never forget my auntie saying, 'You two shouldn't be doing this, you're the babies.' She hated not being able to take care of those things herself. In the end, she just stopped eating – I think she hoped that would bring it on quicker.

She had a hospital bed in her living room at home but woke up one day and decided she wanted to go to the hospice. The whole family went to see her that night. She could hardly talk, but she asked me to sing 'I Will Always

Love You' to her. So, just like I used to do when I was a little girl, I hid behind the curtain in her room and sang for her one last time. I didn't think I'd be strong enough to do it, but I fought my way through the tears and I'm so glad I did.

I was heartbroken when she passed away the next day – 12 October 2004. I went to see her after she'd died to give her a kiss goodbye.

I honestly don't think our family has been the same since. It affected everyone so much and sadly we don't see each other as often as we used to. When I was singing it really brought the family together, but when Steps stopped things weren't the same, and now all my cousins are grown-up and married with busy lives of their own.

Looking back, I think 2004 was probably my toughest year – I wasn't working, my self-esteem had gone AWOL, I was depressed and I was married to a man I wasn't in love with. And, to top it all off, I was getting fat!

Then my lovely auntie passed away and at that point, the realization that you can't be an ostrich your whole life hit me like a ton of bricks. You can't ignore things and hope they'll go away – that's not how the world works. It was like someone had yanked my head out of the sand and said, 'This is all really happening to you. Deal with it.' But I couldn't.

What happened to my Auntie Pauline was a big factor in my decision to leave Mark. She was the first person I was close to who'd died and it became crystal clear to me that life's too short to stay with someone if you're not happy.

I was so upset after she passed away, and Mark eventually told me I needed to pull myself together. I thought, 'Well, actually, I don't.' We kept arguing about different things; then he started saying he wanted to move back up north when I'd told him right from the start that I didn't want to leave London or my family. I'd also been desperate to have a child and always thought that as soon as I got married I'd have one, but I suddenly realized that I didn't want to have a family with Mark. I kept telling him I wasn't ready, but I knew in my heart it wasn't right to have a baby with him.

Mark was very honest about the fact that he wanted a wife who completely adored him and would be the perfect housewife, and I was never going to be that person. I didn't want to spend my life cleaning and cooking for a man. OK, I might not have been working at that point, but I couldn't see myself not working in the future. Apart from anything else I *had* to get back to work – I was running out of money because I hadn't had a job in ages. Every now and then a little payment would come in from Steps or H & Claire, which kept me going, but it wasn't a lot.

Mark was far from happy, too, and one day he just turned round and said, 'Maybe we should have some time away from each other?' I felt relieved that he'd come out and said it, and I knew it was the best thing for both of us.

Around Christmas, he went to stay with his brother up in Leicester for a few days. Christmas was always the time of year that Reece and I texted each other to say hello – but this time I had an overwhelming feeling that I had to talk to him. So I texted, 'Can we talk?' It wasn't for any particular reason; I just really wanted to hear his voice. He called me back later that day.

'I've never stopped loving you, Claire,' he told me. 'I'm sorry for everything that happened and I'm not angry any more that you ended it. I know some of it was my fault.'

I didn't say 'I love you' back, because I was still married to Mark and I didn't want to get myself into something before I'd sorted things out properly with him. But still, my stomach was somersaulting with excitement. Reece and I spoke a few times on the phone after that and he asked if we could meet, but I kept saying no.

In the new year, the whole thing with me and Mark came to a head.

'Can I come home now?' he said, when he called me one day. 'Have you come to your senses?'

'I'm sorry, Mark, but I don't want to be with you any more,' I admitted sadly. After spending some time apart and hearing Reece's voice again, I knew I wanted a divorce and I thought in his heart of hearts Mark probably felt the same.

On Valentine's Day 2005 I went to stay with my mum and, the following day, Mark came over to the house we'd shared, packed up his things and moved out. He called about six weeks later to ask if we could talk and to see, once again, if I'd 'come to my senses', but by then I absolutely knew I'd made the right decision and told him I wanted a divorce.

I was just relieved it was finally over and that I didn't have to be married to him any more. I honestly don't know how it affected Mark and whether he was really cut up about it or not. He probably thought I was a complete bitch, but I know in the long run it was the best thing for me and for him. I don't know his situation now, but I hope he's happy and I hope to God I didn't ruin his life.

I was sorry about what had happened, but the only thing about that relationship I was truly upset about was that I wouldn't be seeing my sister-in-law Bhav any more, because we'd become good friends.

Mark and I had been living in the house I'd bought during my last tour with Steps – where I live with my family today. After I'd quit the band, I'd left it lying empty for months because it needed a lot of work doing to it – it had ivy growing through some of the windows – and I'd been too busy with H & Claire to arrange that.

When Mark and I had moved in we whitewashed the place and fitted wooden floors throughout, which was his style. It was cold and stark and I'd always hated it. As soon as he moved out I decorated the whole place by myself, painting walls red and other warm and vibrant colours. It took me two weeks to do it, but I literally painted Mark out of my life.

7

IT'S THE WAY YOU
MAKE ME FEEL

The week Mark left, Reece and I met for a drink and dinner. I was terrified that he'd think I'd got fat, so I wore a very revealing low-cut top to accentuate the fact that my boobs had got bigger, too. It wasn't all bad news!

'I've put on a bit of weight, but I'm going to go on a diet,' I spluttered out almost as soon as we sat down. I wanted to be the one to acknowledge it before he had a chance to say anything. I was probably a size 14, but I'd make excuses all the time about the shops making clothes smaller and I avoided weighing myself because deep down I knew I was getting bigger.

Even though I'd been really thin the last time we'd been together, Reece clearly wasn't bothered that I was curvier. 'What are you talking about? I think you look great,' he said, smiling back. He seemed to be more than happy with the increase in my cup size!

I spent the rest of the night trying to cover up my boobs

with my big coat because I felt so self-conscious. We had a nice time and the conversation was never stilted – we had so much to talk about. But I deliberately kept things light-hearted because, although I'd separated from Mark, I hadn't seen Reece for a long time and I wasn't sure what I wanted to happen that night. I remember walking from the pub to the Thai restaurant and Reece instinctively took hold of my hand when we were crossing the road – it seemed so natural. When I got in my car to drive home that night, I called him immediately and chatted to him on speaker until I got to my front door. I felt so happy after seeing him.

We met up again and went to the cinema, which was another wonderful evening. I did want him to kiss me that night, but he didn't, so I invited him over to my house for dinner because I thought it was a way of making something happen. When he tried to go home that night we ended up snogging on the doorstep for ages.

'Would you like to stay?' I whispered.

He didn't need asking twice. We slept together that night and it was amazing – just like it had been five years before.

By that point he'd sold his shop and was training to be an electrician. He was meant to be going to college the next day, but he bunked off to stay with me and it was lovely. After that he was at my house pretty much all the time apart from Tuesdays and Saturdays, when he had Olivia and spent the night at Tara's or his mum's. He'd rented his own house out, so it was easy for him to move in with me.

Everything about him being there felt right – it was like

we'd never been apart. I do believe that first time round it was the right person, but the wrong time for both of us. I was so young and he was in a relationship and, after that had finished, I wasn't equipped to deal with the situation. But I'd never fallen out of love with him.

I know this sounds awful because my marriage had literally just ended and it wasn't that I didn't care about that because I did. But I'd known for a long time that I shouldn't have been with Mark. It was so odd that during those five years I was with him I didn't speak to Reece at all or see him; then as soon as my marriage was over we got back together.

When I told my cousin Michelle that Reece and I were a couple again, she said, 'Oh, Mum would be pleased, Claire. She always liked him.' It meant so much that Auntie Pauline would have approved!

Reece and I were so happy being back together and enjoying each other's company that we spent the first few months eating out all the time at TGIs or the Thai restaurant, stuffing our faces with junk at the cinema and having takeaways – basically feeding each other! We both love food and it was fantastic, but unfortunately it had the knock-on effect of making us both bigger, and I got fatter than Reece. I'd regularly make chilli con carne with a family-size pack of mince, pile loads of sour cream and cheese on top and split it equally between myself and Reece. I still had no concept of portion sizes.

For a long time I was confused about why I was putting on weight. When I was with Steps we travelled up and down the country in the Prev, eating really unhealthy service station food: burgers, pasties, bars of chocolate, horrible sandwiches, crisps, cartons of sugary drinks and fizzy pop. That was my staple diet for a long time. I was still eating all of the same things, but I wasn't starving myself half the time like I had been when I was with Steps, and I was far less active.

Living together felt so perfect, though, that after only a few months we went to Tiffany and bought each other commitment rings – just plain bands that we wore on our right hands. I had said to Reece, 'If you ever propose to me, I don't care where you do it or how you do it, but don't do it on my birthday or Christmas because I think that's a cop out!' So of course he did it on Christmas Day in 2005. His reasoning was that because I wouldn't have been expecting it, it would be a really lovely surprise.

I was sitting cross-legged on the floor by the tree opening my presents that morning and happily looking at the concert tickets I'd got, and the few other bits and pieces.

'Come and sit on the sofa next to me,' Reece said.

'No, I'm fine here,' I replied.

Then Reece handed me a medium-sized box and I started to unwrap it. Inside was a smaller jewellery box, which I guessed was earrings. Smiling, I flipped the lid open – and saw a beautiful diamond ring. I was so surprised I was only half aware of Reece getting down on one knee beside me.

'You're my best friend, my soulmate and the love of my

life, and that will never change,' he said. 'So will you make me the happiest man alive and agree to become my wife?' It was a bit awkward because I was still on the floor! We both had a little cry and I don't think I even answered him to start off with because it wasn't a question that needed an answer. It felt so right that we were together and there was no way I was going to say no.

When we went to visit my family at my sister's house that day, no one knew apart from my dad because Reece had asked his permission. Apparently he told Reece, 'You should have done it a long time ago!' So it might not have been Rome and I was wearing my pyjamas, but it was very romantic and I got to tell everyone our exciting news and show off my engagement ring.

After we'd got engaged, Reece and I started to talk about trying for a baby. I used to always say I'd never have a child out of marriage, but my divorce wasn't finalized yet and with Reece it didn't matter; and neither did getting married in a church or having a big flashy wedding. None of those things mattered at all to me as long as we were together.

I was desperate to have a family, but I felt really unhealthy and wanted to lose weight before getting pregnant. The universe had a different plan, though!

In July 2006, Shelina invited me to Ant McPartlin and Lisa Armstrong's wedding as her 'plus one'. We got very drunk at the reception and I'm sure I made a total fool of myself: we were dancing like lunatics to Beyoncé and, unfortunately, when I've had a couple of drinks I think I'm as good a dancer as Shelina! As well as throwing some very bad shapes on the dance floor I'm pretty sure I was talking nonsense all night – all I can hope is that everyone else was as drunk as I was.

It was a really good night and when I got home I said to Reece, 'Right, come on then, let's start trying for a baby now!'

Reece didn't need asking twice and that very night I got pregnant. I've since told Ant and Lisa that they're responsible!

The next morning I felt awful and all my clothes were scattered across the kitchen floor, including TWO pairs of Spanx – a little trick I'd adopted to hide the fact I'd put on so much weight.

My parents' divorce was going through at the same time as my divorce and things started to get a little stressful. Not long after I found out I was pregnant, I completely lost it on the phone with my mum. I'd never had a go at Mum for anything before, but now I found myself screaming into the phone. I don't even remember what I said or why I'd started saying it – it was almost like I'd blacked out.

She was obviously unhappy, but I found what she'd been saying hard to listen to because she compared my divorce to her and my dad's. In my eyes it just wasn't the same – there was no way you could compare thirty years of marriage with what Mark and I had. Our marriage wasn't right from the start and it ended after only eighteen months. And, regardless of how my mum felt about Dad at the time, I still loved him and found their divorce very hard to deal with. My dad was broken for a while, but luckily Gemma was still living with him in the family home and it brought them closer. She looked after him quite a lot.

I just withdrew from it – as usual I hid myself away because I didn't want to confront the fact that our lives had changed and would never be the same again. Whenever Mum or Dad tried to talk to me about their divorce, I'd just shut off. I felt I was still the child and shouldn't have to deal with it. It was selfish of me, but I loved my family so much and they'd always provided that safe place for me to retreat to when the whole Steps thing was going on.

After that row with Mum we didn't talk for three weeks, which was awful. Thankfully my being pregnant gave me the perfect reason to go round with the good news. I'm glad to say that from then on things settled down and it was OK.

My divorce ended up limping on for two years before it was finalized. We tried to make it happen quicker on the grounds of unreasonable behaviour, but the court wasn't having any of it. Our solicitors explained that one of us could admit to committing adultery to move things along, but Mark wouldn't lie. I was fine with saying I'd committed adultery because technically I had – I'd started seeing Reece while I was still married to Mark, but it was a non-starter.

During my pregnancy I just felt absolutely awful all the time. I felt sick constantly and I ate and ate and ate because eating seemed to be the only thing that stopped me from feeling ill once the throwing up stage had finished. The only time I felt normal was when I was eating and, unfortunately, the things I craved were cakes, ice cream and Coke – but it had to be dispenser Coke like the sort you get at McDonald's, not the stuff from a can or a bottle. So I'd go to McDonald's and get four huge cups of Coke in the morning and bring them home and work my way through them during the day. Often I'd go to McDonald's twice in one day – I'd have a huge breakfast of sausage and egg McMuffin with hash browns (and Coke) and sometimes pancakes, too. Then for lunch I'd have a Big Mac with fries, two large Cokes and an apple pie, which I usually had with ice cream. I'd also often buy two McFlurries and stick one in the freezer for later, or I'd go to the cake shop and buy four Yum Yums for 60p and two Belgian buns. I'd eat the Yum Yums before I'd even got home and pretend I hadn't: I'd say to Reece, 'I bought us a treat each, here's your Belgian bun,' after I'd already scoffed the four Yum Yums in the car. I absolutely stuffed my face.

Eating food in secret was a habit I'd got into when I was with Mark, but this was on a much bigger scale. I convinced myself that it was OK to 'eat for two', even though I know a pregnant woman actually only needs an extra 200 calories a day. I thought, 'Well, I'm going to get fat anyway and my body's telling me I need food, so I'll have it.'

To be honest, I found pregnancy a bit of a shock – I'd looked forward to it for so long and I'd seen pregnant women on telly with that healthy glow and just assumed it'd be perfect for me, too. I didn't expect to feel so awful and I'd either not get out of bed at all or just sit on the sofa all day long, which obviously only helped me to pile on more weight. The only time I'd really go out would be in the car – in my pyjamas, with a coat thrown on top – to get my supplies for the day from McDonald's.

I had so little get up and go that my mum began to get quite concerned about me and one day said to me, 'You have to snap out of this, Claire. You're depressed.'

'You don't know how I feel,' I thought. 'If you felt as ill as I do, you wouldn't want to get out of bed either!' It was impossible to be cheerful when I was feeling so sick all the time.

If I wasn't miserable enough before, Christmas only made me sink into an even blacker mood. When I was nearly six months pregnant, Reece went to America to see Olivia, who'd moved out there with her mum. I must have cried all through the Christmas holidays because I felt so ill and missed Reece dreadfully. He'd asked me to go out there with him, but I couldn't even sit on my own sofa for five minutes without feeling sick, so I certainly wasn't going to attempt getting on a transatlantic flight. A little part of me was hoping he'd say, 'OK, then I won't go,' but of course he didn't because he's a great dad and it was important that he saw his daughter.

I was still struggling with the whole step-parent thing: to me it just seemed like he was choosing Olivia over me and our child. But I was incredibly hormonal – I heard myself saying things while I was pregnant that I'd never usually dream of saying. It was like having PMT constantly, but a million times worse, and there was no respite after- wards when you realize you've been really unreasonable – those hormones were raging for the whole nine months!

I was two weeks overdue when I finally went into labour on 8 May 2007 – H's birthday. The birth was pretty trau- matic. The midwife had to break my waters and there was meconium in the fluid, which can be a sign of foetal dis- tress and can lead to breathing problems if the baby inhales it. I was rushed down to the labour ward where they dis- covered the baby wasn't facing the right way and they wanted him to turn by himself, which took ages.

The labour was awful and I was sick several times – once so violently that it splashed back and covered my face and hair! It took two hours to push the baby out because he got stuck in the birth canal and at one point there were three midwives and a doctor with their fingers cupped under his head, trying to ease him out so they didn't have to use forceps.

I barely had time to see that I'd given birth to a boy, my son Charlie, when he was whipped away so they could check on him – they wouldn't even let Reece cut the cord. I was so relieved when I heard Charlie crying and then they passed him to me. He was beautiful and I fell in love immediately

– he had loads of black hair and looked like a little Sumo wrestler because his face was so squashed.

I was taken down to theatre to get a spinal block and to be stitched up, but although I was knackered, I had all this adrenalin rushing through my body and felt really happy that my baby was finally here. There was a radio on and I started singing along to Whitney's 'I Wanna Dance With Somebody', which the staff saw as an invitation to tell me they recognized me. So there I was, singing away, legs akimbo, while they were all staring at my nether regions!

Once the adrenalin left me I felt awful – my hormones were haywire, the stitches were painful, and I was having terrible migraines. The doctor was worried my headaches were caused by a drop in my spinal fluid after the epidural, so I had to stay overnight. Thank goodness I did, because when my baby needed help he got it immediately.

Charlie was in a little cot next to my bed, but at about 1 a.m. he started crying and was inconsolable. His arms had gone stiff out in front of him and his temperature was high, so they whipped him away to the neonatal unit. He was poorly and agitated, but they didn't know exactly what was wrong with him – they thought he had an infection.

I was so upset, the only thing that kept me sane that first night was a tub of chocolate cornflake cakes from M&S, which I worked my way through!

Charlie was moved to a room on his own in case the infection spread to the premature babies. He ended up in the neonatal unit for ten days, and I spent hours every day sitting in a chair by his little cot. It was so strange seeing him among all the tiny preemie babies because he was actually a big bouncing baby – nine pounds four ounces – and looked healthy in comparison.

I really missed out on that precious bonding time with him – although I was a mum, I didn't feel like one. Reece was going home every night and it was heartbreaking that our new little family couldn't be together. Charlie was also receiving antibiotics intravenously and doctors were taking blood from him every day – the poor little thing was like a pin cushion. I remember my sister kept saying to me, 'I don't know how you're coping with this, Claire, I'd be tearing my hair out with worry.' I think instinct just took over and I got on with it because I had to. I'm sure I was in a bit of denial, too, which probably stopped me from falling to pieces.

One day I went down to the unit and they'd given Charlie a dummy, which made breast-feeding difficult from then on. He stopped feeding properly and was losing too much weight, so they put a tube in his nose and Reece and I started syringing milk into it to go into his tummy. It was so scary seeing my baby in that state with a tube in his nose and hooked up to drips. He looked so helpless.

They never got to the bottom of what was actually wrong with him or where the infection was but, thankfully, after ten days he improved and got stronger, and we were allowed to take him home. It was a huge relief.

I managed to breast-feed for three months – I convinced myself that it'd also help me lose weight – but Charlie didn't really take to it and it was a struggle. During that time I just carried on eating junk – anything I could get my hands on, really.

Because I'd missed out on that special bonding time with Charlie when he was born, I became very clingy with him and would just sit and cradle him for hours on end. I never let him out of my sight and there was no way I was going to allow anyone else to look after him. Reece's parents were always asking, 'Can we have him overnight?' and I would always say, 'Why? It's not like we're going out or anything.' I just didn't want to let go of him.

I'd even question Reece's judgement when it came to parenting, and he'd already had a child! I was always saying, 'Why are you doing that?' or 'Don't do it like that, that's wrong.' It must have been difficult for him. I know now that kind of anxiety and overprotectiveness can be a sign of post-natal depression, but at the time I didn't realize this and I never went to the doctor about how I was feeling. Instead, I struggled through and gradually I began to relax a bit more, but I often wonder if that's why Charlie is quite clingy now. He's so sweet and sensitive, and a real Mummy's boy.

After I'd had Charlie and my baby bump had gone, I realized I was still fat, but I didn't do anything about it – I just carried on eating crap day after day. I was so exhausted all the time, as all new mums are, that I convinced myself my body needed all this food for energy. Incredibly, my weight crept up to sixteen and a half stone – the heaviest

I've ever been. I had literally doubled my body weight in the five years since leaving Steps – going from one extreme to the other. But for a long while I was blind to the truth about how big I'd really become.

When I was eating something I loved, I didn't stop when I got to the feeling-full stage – if I was enjoying the taste of something I'd just carry on eating it until it had gone or I physically couldn't eat a mouthful more. For me, food was never to do with satisfying hunger or fuelling my body; it was purely about the pleasure I got from it. I had this compulsion to keep eating – it was like an addiction. And this time round I wasn't starving myself in between binges or making myself sick, and I just got fatter and fatter. In the mornings I'd get up and struggle to walk down the stairs because my ankles hurt so much under the strain of carrying my bulk around, and I had heartburn constantly. In fact, I suffered from acid indigestion so badly, I used to drink Gaviscon straight out of the bottle.

It wasn't just the amount of food I was eating, either – it was the type of food. Unfortunately, all the things I love to eat are packed with fat and calories and contain very little nutrition: burgers, fries, cakes, crisps and ice cream. I'd get takeaways a lot, too, and order as much as possible, and there was never anything left on my plate.

I can really tell the difference when I'm eating well or not eating as much junk because I don't get heartburn and I feel so much better. But back then I just felt horrendous. I was tired all the time, I was constantly hot and sweaty, and would feel out of breath after even the tiniest amount of exertion. I even struggled to sing because I'd get out of breath so quickly. I don't think I could have sung professionally at that point even if I'd wanted to.

I was more self-conscious than ever about my body and I didn't feel feminine at all. I used to buy men's plaid pyjamas in a huge size so every inch of my body was covered up in bed. I liked the fact that the arms and legs were far too long because it made me feel smaller – I could disappear into them. And I lived in men's tracksuit bottoms and hoodies. When I'd been slim, I used to like wearing my boyfriend's sweatshirt because I loved the feeling of it drowning me, but those days were long gone: Reece's clothes would have been tight on me. I remember thinking at the time, 'You're meant to be able to sit on your husband's lap and feel dwarfed and protected by his size,' but I just felt like a huge man sitting on Reece's lap in my tartan PJs!

As far as sex went, it was usually the last thing on my mind if I'm being honest, especially with a new baby. Someone once told me that after giving birth your sex drive disappears for a while so you don't get pregnant again and can focus on nurturing your baby. I don't know if that's an old wives' tale, but I guess I used to make excuses not to have sex. I'd say I was tired because Charlie had been up all night or we couldn't do it because he was asleep in the room with us. And when we did do it, I was far less adventurous – there was no making out in cars and bathrooms!

Reece, on the other hand, could have done it every day and still say it wasn't enough!

The truth was, my body confidence was at rock bottom and I had no energy because I was so big. I still wasn't going out much at all – I'd make excuses not to meet up with friends because I couldn't face the trauma of finding something to wear that actually fitted me and was more glamorous than the leggings and huge oversized sweaters I lived in. If Reece ever complimented me, I just assumed he was lying to make me feel better because I didn't think there was any way he could possibly find me attractive any more. Whenever I looked in the mirror I thought I looked disgusting. On one occasion, when he made a comment about how nice I looked, I lost it a bit.

'Don't lie! Why would you say that? Why are you lying to me?' I snapped at him. Reece insisted he was telling the truth but I simply couldn't believe him.

I tried all sorts of diets, like Slimming World and the Eurodict, but I wouldn't stick to them. I felt so desperate at one point that I went to the doctor.

'Look, I don't know what's wrong with me, because I hate being this fat,' I said, trying to stay calm as I made myself talk about it. 'I can't bear it, but I can't seem to change it. I just can't stop myself eating all the things that are bad for me. Is there a tablet I can take or is there something that can help me?'

I was in floods of tears by the end and literally begging

her to help me, but I don't think she really knew what to say.

'Well, really you just need to go on a diet,' was all that she offered.

Obviously that's common sense, but I just wanted someone to help me to understand why my brain wouldn't allow me to get rid of the thing that was making me the most unhappy – the rolls of fat clinging to my body.

I didn't know what to do or where I was going wrong. I kept thinking that no one in their right mind would be so depressed and upset about being fat that they couldn't leave the house and that every time they had to go out they'd end up crying because nothing fitted and would have to be consoled by their husband. Why couldn't I do anything about it? Why would I still sit there and eat all the stuff that was bad for me?

To Reece's eternal credit, when I was at my fattest, he never once said, 'You need to lose weight' or made me feel unattractive or guilty about the amount of food I was eating. He has always said I'm beautiful. He knew me before I became famous with Steps and he understands what makes me tick. And the difference between him and Mark is that we can talk about absolutely anything – we're best friends. He can also relate more to my struggles with food because he loves all the same things I do – we'd both rather order a curry than make a healthy stir-fry.

A few months after Charlie was born something happened that woke me up to how much I'd changed physically over the past few years. On a rare night out, Reece and I went with H to see Faye perform in *The Eva Cassidy Story*. Afterwards we were all standing in the foyer and some Steps fans came over to us and asked Faye and H for their autographs, but said nothing to me. They didn't know who I was – obviously I was unrecognizable from the Claire Richards they knew from Steps.

I laughed it off, but inside I felt humiliated: it was like a slap in the face. I could feel myself retreating while the others were chatting and signing autographs, and I used it as an excuse to slip away into the background. Part of me didn't want to be recognized anyway, because I was embarrassed by my size. It was so strange – I felt like 'Claire from Steps' on the inside, but no one knew me.

On the way home in the car I couldn't stop thinking about what had happened and kept saying to Reece, 'Surely if you saw someone with two members of Steps who looked a bit like Claire from Steps but fat, wouldn't you think it *was* Claire from Steps?' It really bothered me.

An even bigger reality-check turned up in the autumn of that year in the shape of *Celebrity Masterchef*. It was the first thing I'd been asked to do in ages and I really wanted to take part, but I realized I had nothing to wear to go on telly – my grungy leggings and comfy oversized jumpers wouldn't cut it. I had no choice but to go out and buy clothes, which was something I'd dreaded since putting on weight.

For a long time I'd been trying to convince myself I was a size 16, even though I knew that wasn't true. I was lost in a world of denial. When I started trying things on, the clothes that fitted me were a size 20, although I managed to squeeze myself into a couple of size 18 tops. I remember thinking, 'Do you know what, Claire? You're actually really fat. It's got to stop now!' I was massive. I'd basically been sitting on the sofa for five years eating McDonald's and cakes.

When I saw myself on *Masterchef*, I was horrified. I just thought, 'Oh, my God, I look disgusting!' I hadn't put on much make-up so I was deathly pale, and I'd scraped my hair back into a ponytail, so, not only did I look fat, I looked like I'd made no effort with myself at all. I suppose that dowdy look gave me the anonymity I wanted at the time – I could fade away into the crowd and go unnoticed, but it wasn't a good look for the telly. And, to top it all off, I was still having to wear two pairs of fat pants in an effort to hold everything in!

On a more positive note, I enjoyed doing the show, even though it was quite terrifying, and I made it through to the quarter-finals with a main dish of fillet steak on potato rosti with asparagus, and a cream and mushroom sauce. My dessert was a white chocolate cheesecake with raspberries. And I was so delighted with the comments I got.

'That steak is cooked perfectly,' said Gregg Wallace, the presenter, 'and your mushroom sauce is great. You've cooked everything with an expert touch.'

I couldn't believe it!

Chef John Torode said he was 'impressed' by my main and that I'd plated it up beautifully.

When it came to the cheesecake, Gregg said it was '. . . nigh on perfection. This is what you love doing and it shows so much – it's heavenly,' he added, going in for another spoonful.

John loved my cheesecake, too. 'What you probably should do with that is pack it in little boxes and sell it – it's fantastic!' he said.

'Really? Wow!'

I was so happy, particularly with the comments about my cheesecake – all those Saturdays I'd spent as a kid baking cakes from Mum's cookery books had paid off. It was a real confidence boost and the first positive thing outside family life that I'd experienced in a long time.

And it also made me realize that I had to do something about my weight.

It was the perfect opportunity when, a couple of months later, in January 2008, I was contacted about making a fitness DVD. I also agreed to film a documentary for BBC3 called *My Big Fat Wedding*, which would follow my efforts to lose weight in time for my marriage to Reece on 1 November. After not working for years, I suddenly had all these offers coming in. I was desperate to slim down before my big day and this was my opportunity to get some help to do it.

I do believe very strongly that if you're going to lose weight, it's got to come from you – it has to be your decision to do it. If someone's telling you to do it, nine times out of ten it won't work. You need to want it. The only times I've been focused enough to slim successfully have been when I've had a goal to aim for – when I know exactly where I need to get to and by when.

Often the problem comes once you've reached your target weight and have to maintain it afterwards. That's when a lot of people get into a cycle of yo-yo dieting – overeating, then half starving themselves to make up for it. I've learned only recently that the reason I yo-yo is because I haven't given myself a reason to keep the weight off. As well as setting goals to lose the weight, you must have goals to help you maintain it afterwards.

When I started the diet and exercise plan to slim down for my wedding to Reece, it was because I wanted to do it – luckily for me the show and the DVD came along just at the right time. Every day I had a reason to get out of bed and keep going, not least because the trainer I was working with for the DVD was coming to my house five times a week at one point! I'd dread every session, but afterwards I was glad I'd done it and I felt better for it.

I started off just walking or running on the treadmill – I was so unfit I couldn't do much else at the start. Then I discovered I enjoyed body combat, which involves doing self-defence routines to music. I think it's vital to find a workout you actually enjoy, so you don't get bored and give up.

I used to work out when Charlie was having his nap, but there's no doubt it can be hard finding the time to do it if you're working full-time or are a busy mum, especially when your baby won't play ball and go for his nap. I was lucky because it was pretty much the only thing I had to fit in at the time, but if I'd had to follow that kind of exercise regime by myself, though, I don't know if I could have done it. I'm sure that's why a lot of people work out with a friend – you can motivate each other and are less likely to find an excuse not to do it.

The TV people also sent me to a boot camp in Scotland. I only lost four pounds while I was there, but inches literally disappeared off my hips and thighs because my muscles became really toned. I also followed a healthy calorie-controlled diet, which helped re-educate me about portion sizes. I cut out sugary snacks, booze and my beloved junk food, which wasn't easy, and ate healthy meals such as fish or chicken with vegetables for lunch and dinner.

By the time my wedding came around I was a tiny size 10 again. It had taken about eight months of really hard work and willpower, but I lost a massive six stone: apart from my marriage and my kids, I don't think there's anything I've committed to that religiously! I'd gone from sixteen and a half stone to ten and a half. To be honest, I was a little peeved I hadn't lost more weight until it was explained to me that muscle weighs more than fat and I'd really toned up.

The exercise also completely changed my shape – for the first time in my life I didn't have 'saddle bags' and a bum that spread out! I probably looked thinner at ten and a half stone that I'd looked at nine and a half, and that was down to the exercise. I even had muscle definition in my arms (which I'd never had before); you could finally see my collarbone again and my boobs had returned to their normal size. I felt brilliant and I'd be lying if I said I didn't love looking like that. My tummy will always be wobbly because I have stretch marks from pregnancy, but I could live with that. I only wish I had the gene that makes me want to continue working out like that all the time, but sadly I don't!

Reece was impressed by how dedicated I was and, as much as he'd never say he found me less attractive when I was bigger, it was easier for me to look glamorous and sexy and I'm sure he appreciated that. When you're slim you have more options with clothes, but when you're fat you tend to buy huge things to hide your shape – I certainly did.

Eleven years after we'd first met, Reece and I finally tied the knot on 1 November 2008 at Hampton Court House, a private school in Surrey, with just our close friends and family around us. It was lovely, and a huge contrast to my extravagant stately home wedding to Mark. I absolutely loved it and still feel gutted we're never going to get the chance to do it again!

All of Steps came, which I was so glad about, and Faye sang Eva Cassidy's 'Songbird', which was just beautiful. H had been the only one to attend my wedding to Mark, but I'd only met Reece because I was in Steps so it felt right that the rest of the band was there when I married him.

I slipped into my size 10 Phillipa Lepley dress with ease – it was a really simple, strapless cream gown with gathered silk tulle and an A-line skirt, and I'd bought a diamante brooch to fix to one hip. My friend Jennie swept my hair into an up-do and Jackie did my make-up, giving me sultry, smoky eyes.

I think I always knew I'd end up marrying Reece and I felt very calm during the service, although I did start crying when we were saying our vows because I get so emotional. But I was so happy as I was certain I was doing the right thing: we were always meant to be together. Charlie was a page boy in a little Ralph Lauren suit and Converse trainers. He looked so cute, and sat on our laps as we signed the register.

Everything had been pink and green at my first wedding, but this time I based the theme on a Diptyque candle, so everything was white with hints of black. For a bit of fun I ordered black and white M&Ms as favours with 'Reece and Claire' stamped on every sweet! We had a Frank Sinatra singer at the reception, who was totally brilliant, and people were even up dancing during the meal.

My dad had to make his second 'father of the bride' speech and he did me proud, coming up with a great line: 'This is the third time I've had to do this for Claire,' he said. 'The first one was a tragedy [our families had appeared in the wedding scene of the video for 'Tragedy'], the second was Better Best Forgotten [one of our singles and a reference to my disastrous marriage to Mark] and the third one is a bit of a case of Better The Devil You Know [another of our songs and a reference to Reece].' It was inspired!

The day was brilliant from start to finish and I danced all night long on our multi-coloured light-up dance floor. The DJ played a little Steps medley – 'Let's get this out of the way because everyone's gonna want it!' he shouted over the mic. But his enthusiasm fell flat – no one in the band would get up and dance, and I didn't really want to, either!

For our honeymoon we went to Thailand, and Charlie came with us. It was lovely being away with Reece and Charlie, but I don't have much luck with honeymoons! We went to Koh Samui where it rained for a week and Reece got bitten to death by bugs. So we decided to go to Chiang Mai, where there are no beaches but it's hotter. We checked into a beautiful hotel and tagged a couple of extra days onto our holiday so we could get some sun. On the day we were due to fly back home we got to the airport at 4 a.m. and were told our flight had been delayed – there were actually 75,000 anti-government protesters at Bangkok Airport, and we ended up being stuck in Thailand for an extra ten days!

It was a nightmare, as I was meant to be at home doing a photo shoot for *Now* magazine to accompany a piece on my weight loss with 'before' and 'after' pictures for their January issue. Finally, we managed to get the last two seats on a Korean Airways flight and made it by the skin of our teeth as the gate was closing. By the time we got home it was almost Christmas!

I'd taken all my workout gear to Thailand but probably only managed one gym session in a whole month of being there, so when I got home I'd already put on at least half a stone thanks to discovering a love of Thai food. (In fact, when I did *Celebrity Masterchef* again that autumn – getting to the quarter-finals once again – I made a Thai green curry!). Plus I had been drinking cocktails every night and, every lunchtime, I had ordered a portion of chips on the side. We were on honeymoon, after all!

I still had my trainer because my fitness DVD – *5 Step Fat Attack* – was coming out on Boxing Day, so I was able to shed those extra pounds I'd gained in time for the shoot. And when I was standing in the studio being photographed for the magazine in my tiny size 10 bikini and high heels, I felt pretty bloody good! It had been a monumental effort, but it had paid off. And I'd done it without starving myself – it was all down to a sensible eating plan with lots of healthy food and a lot of hard work in the gym!

The DVD was an instant hit and ended up being the best-selling fitness DVD of 2009. I think people were genuinely amazed by the change in my body from looking at the 'before' and 'after' shots and hopefully thought, 'Well, if she can do it, so can I.'

I carried on working out with my trainer into the new year, but after he'd gone, I have to admit I was less motivated to exercise and the pounds did start to creep on again. I went to an award ceremony in February and had my picture taken standing next to actresses Daniella Westbrook and Adele Silva. The next day the papers were full of stories that I'd already started putting on weight again. I was only a size 12 and not fat by any stretch of the imagination, but when standing next to Daniella and Adele, who are both tiny, tanned and about six inches shorter than me, I probably did look like an elephant!

A couple of months after we got married, Reece and I hit a bit of a rocky patch, but we handled things very differently this time round and decided to go to Relate for counselling. It was partly do to with the fact that my sex drive had gone AWOL for a while after I'd had Charlie, but also because I still didn't know how to cope with being a stepmum and didn't understand where my place was in the grand scheme of things. I didn't know where I fitted into the strong little family unit of Reece, his parents and Olivia.

Whenever Olivia was with us I felt I should be a figure of authority because she was staying in my house, but I was probably a bit hard on her. She was quite a fussy eater and I tried to encourage her to eat other things, but everyone else would just let her have what she wanted. They were used to giving into her and it really bothered me. Reece had dated a woman called Marianna for about a year and Olivia was always saying to me, 'Oh, well, Marianna gave me that' or 'Marianna did this', so there was a bit of a power struggle for a while.

I felt on the outside of things for a long time and eventually, because I wasn't Olivia's mum, it started to seem as if I had no right to assert any kind of authority in my own home.

I realized that Reece and I had to sit down and talk through it all with someone who understood those issues and could help us to understand where each other was coming from. And so we went to Relate.

By going to Relate, I came to realize that I had to take a step back because I'm not Olivia's mum – I'll never have that relationship with her – and I accepted that it's not really my responsibility to make decisions for her. Reece is her dad – it's up to him to sort out what she's eating and drinking. At the same time, Reece had to learn not to undermine me all the time when it came to my relationship with Olivia.

When we got married, Olivia was at a difficult age – it was just before her tenth birthday and she'd had many years of having her dad to herself. I think Reece, too, was still carrying around a lot of guilt about leaving when she was a baby so he could be with me. He had never wanted to leave Olivia – never ever – which was why he couldn't commit to me at first and why we had kept breaking up every five minutes.

In fact, both of us were still carrying around a lot of baggage from our affair that we hadn't really dealt with. The counselling we got at Relate really was helpful and I'm glad to say things started to work much better afterwards. I stopped involving myself in some things to do with Olivia and there was also a bit more give and take from everyone. Gradually, I began to work out where I fitted in.

Reece and I had been trying for another baby and, in April 2009, I was delighted to find out I was pregnant again. The two-year age gap between Charlie and his new brother or sister seemed perfect. And this time I planned to keep exercising throughout my pregnancy to avoid piling on loads of weight like I'd done when I was having Charlie. However, by the time I was six weeks into the pregnancy, I could barely stand up in the morning because I felt so ill. If I even tried to do a squat I felt like throwing up!

I assumed I was having another boy because I felt exactly the same – ill all the time – but this time I had a toddler to look after into the bargain. As well as feeling sick, I also had a horrible taste in my mouth the whole time, too, and the only way to get rid of it was to eat, so about six weeks in, that was it – I started eating A LOT and the only exercise I got was running round after Charlie.

The first twelve weeks were pretty miserable, and even though I did improve a bit after that, I still felt nauseous for almost my entire pregnancy – right up until the last few weeks. But at least I was a bit more relaxed the second time around. I didn't worry so much and I'd have a peanut M&M or a little bit of wine or Guinness on a special occasion.

My baby was due on Christmas Day but was late once again, so, to keep myself busy over the holidays and my mind off the impending birth, I made about seven

Christmas cakes to give to people as gifts, as well as jars and jars of mincemeat and lots of coconut ice, which I put in old-fashioned candy jars and tied up with ribbon. And I cooked me and Reece a huge Christmas dinner.

Daisy arrived four days late on 29 December and Reece and I were both thrilled to have a little girl and a sister for Charlie. Thankfully, the birth was far less traumatic than Charlie's and she fed straightaway. She was so sweet and pretty, and I was so excited that my world was about to turn pink! When we took Daisy home and introduced Charlie to her she was crying, so he ran to his playroom and came back with his toy keyboard, and began singing, 'Daisy, Daisy'. Now whenever she's upset or having a tantrum, we all sing Charlie's little song!

When the baby bump had gone, I was still fat – just like I'd been after having Charlie. I hadn't put on quite as much weight with Daisy as I had with my first pregnancy, although it was probably more than I admitted to at the time! When I had her, I was about fourteen and a half stone: I had been around twelve stone when I'd got pregnant. But, after the birth, I carried on 'eating for two' and, once again, my weight started to creep up, this time to just under fifteen stone.

I couldn't believe I was back in this position again – seriously overweight and unable to stop myself from eating junk.

8

A SLAVE TO FOOD

'I can't believe I have to do this again!' I wailed. It was January 2010 and I was on the phone to my agent Neil Howarth. I'd signed up with him in 2008 and now he was calling to see if I was interested in doing another diet to lose my baby weight, this time with *Closer* magazine. The aim was to slim down to a size 10 in time for a bikini shoot towards the end of the year.

At first, I just couldn't face the thought of it – I was really annoyed with myself for putting on so much weight again. My heart sank every time I thought of what it would take to lose five stone, which was what I needed to do to get down to a size 10. It would be mentally as well as physically challenging, and I knew I had to be in the right place to do it. I can totally understand why so many very overweight people start diets and don't see them through, because the enormity of what you have to accomplish is mind-blowing. When I was at my biggest after having Charlie, I lost six stone – that's the equivalent weight of a small person!

Nevertheless, I knew I had to do it and I needed help to achieve it. This time, though, I was determined to take a bit longer – I wanted to do it on my terms. When I was trying to lose weight after having Charlie, I'd go to parties and not drink alcohol and I wouldn't go near the buffet table, but this time I just thought, 'Don't worry, don't give yourself a hard time; you'll get there eventually. If it takes a year, that's OK.'

They wanted me to start the diet and exercise plan straightaway, but it hadn't been that long since Daisy was born and I wanted to focus on her and not have to worry about a strict diet and fitness regime. And it did pretty much take a year, because I was less religious with my diet – I allowed myself the odd takeaway or a glass of wine. But it felt right to take things a bit more slowly.

With the help of a nutritionist, I shrank my portion sizes and followed a healthy diet, which involved no more than 1,500 calories a day. I cut out treats (apart from the occasional bag of Maltesers!), and did my best to avoid finishing off Charlie's leftovers.

I also started training with Lee, who'd become a successful fitness coach after Steps broke up. It was the best we'd ever got on – once we were out of the pressure-cooker that was Steps, we could be mates and it was nice. We'd spent so long not speaking to each other when we were in the band, so it was brilliant being able to spend some time together now. He came over to my house three or four times a week for months and I did everything he asked me to do. I really tried hard and put in the hours – I think he was quite surprised by that. We both enjoyed it and we became proper friends.

Lee is very good at his job – he obviously knows his stuff, and was really good at devising routines that would fit in with my lifestyle. I did kickboxing to tone up and I ran on the treadmill for about forty minutes every day, which was a great calorie burner.

Not long after I'd embarked on the weight-loss plan for *Closer*, I was contacted by the TV channel Sky Living to find out if I'd be interested in making a documentary series called *Slave To Food*. They wanted to follow me while I attempted to lose weight for the swimwear shoot and to carry on filming me afterwards to see how I coped on my own once that goal had gone and the nutritionists and trainers had left. It was an interesting idea, so I signed up – now I had TV cameras following my every move!

As I had known it would, I did take longer to lose the weight this time around, but by March 2011, my newly slim and sexy body was ready for its close-up!

When I came to shoot the pictures for *Closer* magazine I was ten and a half stone, but I didn't look as small as I did when I'd dieted before my wedding – I think going to that boot camp in Scotland after I had Charlie made a huge difference to my body shape. But I felt really good about how I looked and I'd achieved what I'd set out to do – I'd lost a whopping five stone of takeaways, McDonald's and baby weight through sheer hard work and willpower!

My 'before' pictures were a bit more glamorous this time, which I was grateful for. Normally you're made to look as crap and as miserable as possible, looking down for the full double-chin effect! On the day of the 'after' shoot, though, I was adamant that I wouldn't wear a bikini. I'd had another child and I knew I'd just feel more comfortable in a one-piece, so I posed in a variety of swimsuits.

A couple of the girls on the shoot were caught on camera saying there was no way I was a size 10 but, believe it or not, I didn't take it to heart. I was a bit irritated, but I just thought, 'You know what, I've worked really hard and I think I look bloody good.' Admittedly, the dress I wore for one of the pictures was a size 12, but there were two huge bulldog clips pulling it in at the back because it was too big for me.

I'm sure if I had been a lot bigger and someone had made those comments it would have upset me a lot more, but I'd lost a hell of a lot of weight and I looked and felt slim. I was happy and proud of the work I'd put in and that was what counted. And I think if you put yourself in a mag in a swimsuit, you're fair game anyway – if I'd worked in an office full of women I'm sure there would have been someone who'd have a negative opinion about the way I looked, too.

*

When it came to *Slave To Food* I didn't want the show to just be about how I lost the weight in the same way as *My Big Fat Wedding*. This time, I really wanted to delve a bit more deeply into why I had such a complex relationship with food and why I'm unable to keep the weight off once I've lost it. I wanted to find out why it happens to me and not to other people – like my sister, for example. I'd got to the point where I was convinced there was something terribly wrong with me – there had to be a reason why I couldn't stop yo-yoing.

As part of the show I went to see a doctor – again, I was looking for the magic answer. I wanted her to tell me I had some faulty gene or hormone that could be treated and that all my problems would be solved. But of course it wasn't that simple.

Having talked to a few experts on the show, I believe strongly that the reasons why people overeat are complex and psychological, and unless you get to the root of those and accept what you're like as a person, nothing can change. I have an emotional connection to food – I eat when I'm happy; I eat when I'm sad; and I don't know when to stop if I'm enjoying it.

Someone who helped me unravel my relationship with food while I was making *Slave To Food* was Mike Weeks, the coach who'd previously helped Jack Osbourne to lose weight. He believes my weight issues all stem from my crippling lack of self-confidence and my tendency to worry too much about what people think of me. I had told him about looking at nasty comments left on a newspaper website from readers who were all having a go at me for being fat and Mike just said to me, 'Why do you care so much what complete strangers with too much time on their hands think of you?'

As a confidence-building exercise, he made me walk up to total strangers in a busy London street and pretend I knew them; and it was all captured on film for *Slave To Food*. Gulp! I was bloody terrified!

'Go on, Claire,' he said, giving me a gentle push in the direction of the first passer-by.

'Sarah, right?' I called out to this poor woman. 'Didn't you live next door to Gemma Richards?'

'Er, no,' she said smiling. 'I think you've got me confused with someone else.'

I felt like such a berk, but the more I did it, the less bothered I was about what these people would think of me when I walked away. Mike's theory is that if you can make mistakes without dwelling on negative emotions afterwards, then life becomes easier. I know he's right and I do worry less now about how others perceive me.

And I understand how my lack of self-confidence meant I was always comparing myself to other women: in Steps I constantly compared myself to Faye and Lisa. Growing up, I probably compared myself to my sister Gemma on a subconscious level. She was always so tiny and thin and, even though I wasn't a fat child, I was always the bigger sister

– in size as well as age. And I always had a much bigger appetite.

There's a phrase that goes: 'Some people eat to live and some people live to eat', and I'm obviously the latter. But I'd give my right arm to be the first one! Jackie only eats what's good for her and she sees food as a means of fuelling her body to keep her going. She doesn't have that emotional connection to food that I do.

Food for me is almost like a drug – I get an instant gratification from it, but it doesn't last very long, so then I have to find the next thing to eat to satisfy my craving. You could compare it to being a drug addict or an alcoholic, I suppose.

I know there will be plenty of people out there who believe there's no such thing as food addiction, but I don't agree. I find comfort and pleasure in food and I find it very hard to stop eating those things that will make me fat. I eat purely with my taste buds instead of my brain – I used to stuff food down so fast I wouldn't realize I was full up until it was too late. It was all about satisfying my craving for the taste of something. I was ridiculously excited when Häagan-Dazs ice cream first came to this country because I'd spent so many years as a kid watching American TV where the characters on shows would sit on the sofa, eating ice cream straight out of the tub! For me, there's something wonderful about scooping ice cream out of a tub in front of the telly – I just love it.

But although food gives me so much pleasure, it's also the thing that can make me feel the lowest. After a big takeaway or McDonald's binge I'd feel so down and immediately think, 'Why did I eat that? I should NEVER have eaten that,' and I'd give myself a really hard time for it. And, as well as feeling mentally low, I'd also feel terrible physically because I was so nauseous and bloated. When I was in Steps I used to feel that same crushing low after eating stuff that was bad for me, and as we've seen, in those days I'd starve myself afterwards or make myself sick sometimes. But when I was sixteen and a half stone, the only thing that would make that awful feeling go away was having more food.

If I had even a penny for every single time I've said, 'That's it, I'm not eating that again' or 'I'm going on a diet' I'd be a rich woman. But one of the things I learnt from making the series was that I'm not the only one who has those feelings, and that was a real comfort.

The response I got from people who'd seen me on *Slave To Food* was amazing and really touching. So many women – and men – wrote to me, saying they thought I was brave for making the programme and being so honest about my issues with food, and that they felt exactly the same way. One woman even said that when she saw me talking about my problems, 'it was like looking in the mirror'. And quite a lot of the letters started off along the lines of, 'I'd never normally write to a celebrity, but . . .' These people obviously felt so strongly about the issues I'd tackled in the show and that gave me a real boost, because I knew I wasn't battling these feelings alone. There are more people like me out there than I ever realized.

I was also glad I was able to show that not everyone in the celebrity world is perfect – far from it; they just hide their imperfections really well! But that's not what the music industry would have you believe. As part of the series, I went to see a woman who was involved in promoting girl bands and asked her outright if she'd put me in one of her bands looking the way I did then (at this point in the show I'd already started to put on a bit of weight again). She thought about it for a minute – obviously trying to work out how to be tactful – then said, 'No, I wouldn't. Not when the rest of the band are all young, sexy girls that look hot.'

'So, can you not be hot if you're a size 12 or 14?' I asked.

'Not if the others are all a size 8,' she replied.

'Is it impossible to find a line-up of girls who are all a size 12?' I pushed her.

But she wasn't really getting the point I was trying to make. It was clear to me that in the ten years since leaving Steps, nothing had changed in the music industry. In the pop world, image comes before anything else most of the time and, regardless of my talent, she wouldn't have considered me for a band because I wasn't thin enough.

It didn't really surprise me because after I'd left Steps and put on weight I'd go to meetings about recording contracts and I would see instantly in people's faces that I was never going to hear from them again because of the way I looked. It wasn't because I couldn't sing – it was because I wasn't 'Claire from Steps' any more.

It was depressing because I was desperate to sing professionally again. It had been a part of my life for as long as I could remember and I really missed it. But, the fact was, I'd lost my confidence – for the past few years I'd been at home being a mum and, while my other band members had carried on working, I'd been on the sofa stuffing my face. The thought of auditioning when I wasn't a size 8 filled me with dread.

Something that gave me a real boost, however, was doing a mock audition for a West End casting director as part of the show – maybe the pop world wouldn't have me, but musical theatre might be something I could do?

As usual, I was bloody nervous and was finding it hard to get going, so the casting director told me to block everything out and put my hands over my eyes, then take them away and start singing like I was making my comeback and emerging from the little bubble I'd been in for the past few years. It sounds bonkers, but it really worked! I sang 'As If We Never Said Goodbye' from *Sunset Boulevard*.

I was so choked up towards the end because I really felt every single word of the lyrics. I wanted to get back to performing, I really did, but I couldn't do it if my weight rocketed again. I could barely catch my breath when I'd been sixteen stone, and I knew I wouldn't be able to sing properly. Added to this, for *Slave To Food* Mike Weeks actually made me wear a vest that weighed four stone, and do a dance routine to make me see that, physically, I wouldn't be able to do it if I put on that much weight again. It was so heavy I couldn't actually believe I used to carry all that bulk around – I could barely walk, let alone dance. No wonder my ankles had seized up!

And I really didn't want to ever have to face losing all that weight again. It's bloody tough when you have several stone to shed! I wanted to be able to say, 'I'm not going on a diet any more.'

Before making *Slave To Food*, I felt pretty desperate and assumed I'd be trapped in a cycle of yo-yo dieting for the rest of my life. But the experts I met on the show helped me see things differently. Now I don't feel like that – I can see that keeping my weight steady is about making small, achievable changes to my diet day to day, so I don't pile on six stone and end up having to lose it all again.

I'm the classic yo-yo dieter – losing weight then putting it on again, always looking for the miracle plan that will help me drop dress sizes instantly with little or no effort, while still eating all of those naughty things I love.

It's so easy to be lured in by the diet industry – every week you pick up a magazine and there's another new diet promising the impossible. I understand now that staying slim is about eating a healthy diet and doing a bit of exercise – and that's it! It's not about what blood type you are, or eating protein but not carbs. It's just about being sensible and educating yourself about portion sizes.

But it's very hard to do when you're so desperate you'll try anything to drop pounds fast. I know that more than anyone. Since joining Steps, I've tried pretty much everything going – barely eating anything at all, Atkins and detox – along with cupping, acupuncture, and machines that claim to melt fat! I was always trying a new fad, but they never lasted long. What works is controlling calories sensibly. There are no shortcuts. It takes effort and it can be boring, but if you accept that's what you have to do, then you'll get results. And once you do get to a stage where you are slimmer, your weight becomes easier to control because you've got into good habits. You can still eat the things you like, as long as you're watching portion sizes and calories.

Doing the show also made me more able to accept what I was like as a person. For years I wouldn't really face up to the fact that I had problems with food – I was my own worst enemy a lot of the time. And it helped me like myself more, too, so I stopped giving myself such a hard time. I could see that I don't have to be skinny to look good – which is what I'd thought the entire time I was in Steps – and that I can look attractive when I'm bigger.

I'm not saying it's OK to be fat, because it's not, and that's just as bad for you as being anorexic. But I know now I can look good at a size 14 or even a 16, as well as a size 10. In the past, being a size 14 or 16 would have made me utterly miserable and I wouldn't have wanted to leave the house, but now I'm OK with it. I know now that tent-like clothes only make me looking bigger and that form-fitting dresses will actually show off my small waist and make my curvy figure look better. I think I've managed to get past the point where I'll sit at home and get upset and depressed about being bigger than a size 10 or 12. I'm learning to be happy with, and accept, my shape. I reckon for some people I'll always be 'the fat one from Steps' and that'll never change, but these days I'm a lot further down the road to thinking 'Sod them!' What counts is how I feel inside.

The show also made me finally accept that my husband Reece really does love me regardless of what size I am. As I've already mentioned, when I was a size 20 he'd tell me all the time how beautiful I was and how much he loved me, and he never once made me feel self-conscious, but at the time I could never quite believe him.

In one of the episodes of the show he said, 'Claire still doesn't realize how talented and beautiful she is.' He's the kind of guy who's always joking around – he'll say something nice and follow it up with a sarky comment, but to hear him say that on camera was so lovely. And he's kept that story up for seven years now, so I guess I should accept that it's how he really feels! But I always joke that his rose-tinted specs are going to fall off one day and he'll get the shock of his life!

It also meant a lot to me that he said he thought I was a talented singer, because I respect his opinion. It was a real confidence boost, and it came just at the right time because another opportunity was about to present itself.

While I was still filming *Slave To Food*, my agent Neil asked me if I'd be interested in auditioning for the next series of ITV1's *Popstar To Operastar*. It's an *X Factor*-style talent show where established pop singers learn to sing opera and there's a public vote at the end of each show.

I didn't have to think twice – I really, really wanted to do it. It was all about singing; there was no dancing, no bandmates, and it didn't matter if I was carrying a few extra pounds! I was so excited at the audition because I wanted it so badly.

'Don't get your hopes up too much, in case you don't get it,' warned Neil. 'There are other people in the frame and I don't want you to be disappointed.'

He was right and I'd been disappointed in the past when things didn't come off, so I tried to put a bit of a wall around me in case it didn't happen.

When Neil called on Good Friday to let me know I'd been picked, I was excited beyond belief – and then I panicked immediately, of course! It hit me that I was actually going to have to come up with the goods now, and I hadn't sung on telly for a very long time. But I didn't have much time to stew on it because within days I was whisked off to the studios to meet my mentor, Katherine Jenkins, and to be given my first song – and it was all being filmed for the show.

'Would you mind singing me something, Claire, so I can hear your natural voice?' said Katherine, giving me an encouraging smile. She wanted to hear what I was capable of.

'Er, yeah, no problem,' I stammered, but it took me fifteen minutes to pull myself together enough to sing a few bars of 'Tragedy', as Katherine looked on bemused. I was convinced she was thinking, 'For God's sake, you're meant to be a singer!' but she was lovely to me, and tried to help me feel at ease.

There were loads of other people in the room who I didn't know, staring at me and waiting for me to sing, and I just got cold feet. Eventually, however, I broke the uncomfortable silence and sang, and it was fine – but my lack of self-confidence had got the better of me once again.

'You're so talented,' Katherine said after I'd finished. 'You can do this, but you have to believe it or it'll hold you back.'

After I'd done the *Closer* shoot, I had gone back to being on my own again as far as my diet went, which only meant one thing – I'd started to put on some weight again. Lee wasn't coming over to my house three or four times a week any more to make me exercise, so I'd stopped doing it, even though I knew I should keep it up. It was hard to find the motivation and the time when I was juggling looking after the kids with work. So when I turned up for *Popstar To Operastar*'s launch and saw that one of the Pussycat Dolls, Melody Thornton, was also a contestant, I had a moment of thinking, 'Shit!' As you'd expect, she was very glamorous and tiny. Cheryl Baker from Bucks Fizz was on the show as well, and she was thinner than me, too, because she'd been promoting all the Jenny Craig diets.

I'd found a dress I was happy with that made me look slim, but it was a little tight and my bum felt a bit exposed. The stylist decided to put ribbon on it to tie the back up, so while everyone else had these beautiful dresses that fitted them like a glove, I had to get a bloody big bow attached to mine! I was a size 12–14 at the time so after that they got me size 14 dresses and took them in a bit on the bust. But none of the papers commented on my weight, so luckily I was able to just forget about it and focus on my singing.

I loved the glamour of the show – all the gorgeous gowns and the extravagant hair and make-up. I let them do whatever they wanted to me, so I always had a big mad hairdo!

For my first performance on 12 June I sang 'O Mio Babbino Caro' from *Gianni Schicchi* by Puccini. I was wearing a long yellow gown. I was so terrified that I was visibly shaking but, when I'd finished singing, the whole audience stood up and applauded, and I couldn't hold back my tears – the floodgates had opened!

It was a very emotional moment for me because it was the first time I'd sung in public in a very long time. The past ten years had been building up to that moment and having the audience react like that just got to me – I enjoyed making the show so much and I loved the training. It was so good for me. For a long while I'd been worried that my voice had gone, but this proved it was still there and it gave me a massive confidence boost.

When I was a kid, a vocal coach had wanted to train me as an opera singer – I was only about fourteen at the time and I kind of dismissed it, probably because I didn't think it was 'cool' enough. But I wish I hadn't, especially after people on the show said I could sing opera; that I had the range and the depth in my voice to be able to do it. I got some amazing comments from the judges and it was wonderful to be praised for something I loved doing so much. And oh my God, the calibre of people telling me I could be an opera singer was extraordinary: classical singer, Katherine Jenkins; actor and opera director, Simon Callow; tenor Rolando Villazón; and violinist Vanessa-Mae. I had never realized I could hit the notes I was hitting! One of the teachers even said, 'You're not a belter, you're a soprano', which I was chuffed about after Steps, where I was always thought of as the one in the band who could belt out songs – the one with the 'powerful' voice.

It was lovely for my family, too, because the old groupie gang got back together to come and watch me perform: Mum, Auntie Chris, my dad and Reece. My dad could never cope with watching me when I was in Steps because he'd get so nervous, but he came almost every week to see me in *Popstar To Operastar*. He always had a little tear in his eye – he was very proud of me.

Doing the show was wonderful for so many reasons, but what it did more than anything else was to help me realize that I have to sing if I want to be happy.

9

BACK TOGETHER

'Push your hip up a bit more, Claire. Now, look at me. That's it! You look great, you look FABULOUS!' shouted the photographer, as Abba blared from the speakers and an army of stylists, hair and make-up artists and assistants buzzed around behind him.

The photographer, David Venni, was trying to help me relax while he snapped away – quite a tall order as I was lying butt-naked on the floor of a studio in central London. I had only a pair of super-high strappy stilettos and some bangles to protect my modesty, and they weren't doing a very good job!

It felt a very long way from the Uxbridge school run: only an hour before I'd been running around my kitchen in leggings and a hoodie, making toast and cereal for the kids and frantically trying to get them organized for the day, searching for hair bobbles and water bottles.

In the three or four months since doing my big reveal

shoot for *Closer* after shedding five stone to get down to a size 10, I'd put on weight again and was back to being a size 14–16, and weighed around twelve stone. But, actually, I didn't feel bad about it. I didn't want to get any bigger, of course, but I felt OK with how I looked. I was in a very good place – I was loving my time on *Popstar To Operastar,* and making *Slave To Food* did a lot to improve my body confidence. I felt happier in myself than I had in a long time.

Closer magazine had asked me to be photographed again, but this time naked – as a celebration of my curves, and to prove to other women with a normal body shape like mine that you don't need to be a size 8 to be attractive and sexy.

At first I wasn't sure about it – after all, I'd spent years trying every trick in the book to cover up my bum. Now it would be there in all its glory, completely starkers in a magazine for the entire world to see. In fact, David was convinced I'd never agree to it. 'I know her and she won't do it,' he'd insisted, so he was more shocked than anyone when I said I was up for it.

After all my struggles with body image I felt it was an important thing to do – not just for myself, but for other women, too. In the past I'd been criticized for being too big, even when I was a size 12, so with this photo I wanted to make the point that I'm just one of many women in the UK who's a size 14–16, and I'm not fat, I'm average. OK, I'm not toned and I'm not a size 10 any more and, yes, my weight has yo-yoed over the years but, actually, I know I can dress up to go out and I'll still look good. So, I took a deep breath, hoped I wouldn't regret it, and put the date for the photo shoot in my diary.

I was keen for David to take the pictures because I'd worked with him during the early days of Steps: not only is he a great photographer, but I trust him and knew I'd feel less self-conscious if he was behind the camera. He's also full of banter and we'd be able to have a laugh while we were doing it.

We copied a shoot that plus-size model Crystal Renn had done and I was pleased with the results. I'm lying on my side, propping my head up in one hand with my other arm covering my boobs, my top leg curled up to make sure nothing else is on show! It's a nice picture – OK, there are a couple of little spare tyres, but I don't think I look fat.

I guess what I hadn't thought about properly was the impact the photograph might have! It appeared in *Closer* first, but then to my shock the *Sun* picked up on it and there I was, lying naked on the centre spread of a national news-paper read by millions! I'd actually forgotten to tell my dad I was doing it so when he saw the paper he left me a funny voicemail saying, 'I've seen the paper, Claire. You're a very naughty girl!' Reece liked it, too, although he thought it made me look bigger than I actually was.

I'm genuinely proud of that photo as I think it does prove a point for curvy women. I've had two kids, so of course I've got a bit of a flabby bum and tummy. I wanted to do something to celebrate the female body, to show what a real woman's body looks like. It's sad that a waif-like figure with no hips or boobs has become the ideal for young girls to aspire to as there are very few women who naturally have that shape. It isn't the norm – if you were to line up every woman in Britain you'd soon see what the average figure looked like, and it would be a lot more like mine than Kate Moss's!

The response I got to the picture was unbelievable. I was interviewed on Skype for the *Tonight Show* in the US. I think they were shocked that someone with my background had been brave enough to do it – someone whose career had depended on looking slim and being that perfect 'cookie cutter' pop star. And so many women tweeted and sent messages to thank me for doing it. The *Sun* even did a follow-up piece with three readers posing naked in the style of my photo, and they all said that if I hadn't been photographed like that, they would never have felt brave enough to show their bodies and feel proud of them.

The fact is, in this country the average size for a woman is a 16. Now, if that's average, how can it be fat? But in the industry I work in, it is considered fat because nine times out of ten you're standing next to someone who's a size 8 or smaller. You're going to look enormous next to someone that small.

At the other end of the scale there are women in the public eye like Dawn French – she was very big, and seemed to take the line that she loved being fat. I don't really believe people when they say they're happy being fat, but I do think there's a balance and that it's dangerous to place everything on your weight and how you look. Of course, Dawn has now slimmed down and looks fantastic – and happy, too.

When I did the naked shoot I was still in the middle of *Popstar To Operastar*. On 3 July I had to sing 'The Queen Of The Night' aria from *The Magic Flute* by Mozart for a place in the final. It was an ambitious song choice as it has some incredibly high notes and you have to control your breathing really well to get through it. In rehearsals Rolando was amazed: 'No pop star has ever attempted such high notes,' he said. It was a whole octave – and a bit! – higher than 'Tragedy'. I never knew I was capable of it. It was my best performance without a doubt and when the judges came to give their comments afterwards, Simon Callow said, 'I was absolutely stunned. There are only twelve singers in the world who can sing that aria and you're one of them.' It was such a huge compliment.

Sadly, I was beaten to a place in the final by Cheryl Baker, and she lost out to *X Factor* winner Joe McElderry, who won the show.

The day after I was voted out I felt pretty devastated; I think I cried for most of it, which is ridiculous! And, actually, I never expected to win – I always thought Joe would do it. I'd just enjoyed the show so much and knew I was going to really miss it. It had been an amazing experience. My disappointment didn't last long, though, as I was getting a lot better at bouncing back from rejection!

★

By this point, there was something else in the pipeline – something big! While I was filming *Slave To Food*, the idea of a Steps reunion documentary was being bandied about. I'd been speaking to Faye, Lisa and Lee for a while now – they'd all come to our wedding and, of course, Lee had trained me after I'd had Daisy. And I'd always stayed in touch with H.

We'd all had separate conversations over the years about Steps, but we'd never sat down together and talked about the past or about a future for the band. We'd been asked many times to get the group back together, but it had never happened for one reason or another – either someone wasn't able to fit it into their schedule, or it hadn't felt like the right offer. We were asked to close club night G.A.Y. at the Astoria on Tottenham Court Road, as the building was being knocked down as part of a redevelopment project. We talked about that for a while, but H wasn't really up for it, so we decided not to do it. It would have been great, though, because that place held a lot of memories for us and we had a lot of gay fans.

I think we all wanted to make sure that if we did get back together for a project, it wouldn't be something that would damage Steps' legacy. I know 'legacy' sounds like a very important and dramatic word, but we'd split up at the top of our game – we'd just finished a sell-out arena tour and had a number-one album – so to do it in the wrong way would have been a huge mistake. Whatever anyone thought of our music, there was no denying that in our day we were huge, and none of us wanted to taint that memory, I suppose. We were also aware that lots of other bands had tried and failed to make a comeback, including Blue and All Saints.

It would be hard to emulate the kind of success we'd had, and we wanted to make sure that if we did anything at all, it would be big enough to justify doing it.

We kept getting an offer from Sky for a 'Steps, The Docu-Musical' type of show, which started life as a one-off, then went to two episodes and then three. It was basically a kind of glamorous *Glee*-style documentary about Steps where every now and again we'd just spontaneously burst into song! All of us were like, 'Oh, for God's sake, that's AWFUL!' so we kept saying no to it.

I suppose I was the one to push for us to do something at the start. It was coming up for the tenth anniversary of the band splitting up and we'd heard that Sony, which owns our back catalogue, was going to put out a greatest hits album. Normally, that kind of thing sinks without a trace, so we all decided that if the record company was going to do something, then we should think about supporting it and getting involved. Our old manager Tim Byrne was up for managing us and I thought it was a good idea, but obviously I had to make sure H was OK with it – he'd split up with Tim five or six years before and now had a new partner. Plus Tim works with Simon Cowell at SyCo, so I thought that could put us in a brilliant position – we thought we might even get an *X Factor* performance out of it!

We were all a bit wary of doing any kind of TV show – we weren't sure whether it was the right thing to do and how involved we should be. These days everything's about reality shows because they're so successful, so we had the idea of doing a one-off, Take That-style documentary, which would go on air at the same time the album was released. It would just be us, talking honestly about our story together for the first time.

Sky reappeared with their idea, but it was more along the lines of *The Only Way Is Essex*. I decided I didn't want to do it, partly because I felt it would be wasted on a digital channel: I was convinced that for it to be the success we'd always talked about, we needed to get it out there to as many people as possible.

I had a chat with Tim on the phone at the time and told him my worries, one of which was that they wanted to put us in situations where we'd be asked uncomfortable questions that we'd have to answer. Being a person who would rather cut off her right arm than discuss difficult stuff I panicked, I suppose. I just didn't want to be made to look like the bad guy, which I felt was a possibility because I'd walked out of the band first. I knew the others would want to press H and me on why we'd left and, although we'd discussed it separately over the years and it had been fine, we'd never talked about it all together in one room. I was worried I wouldn't be able to get my point across properly. I also had other work commitments so I was concerned about how long it would take to film a series, rather than just the one-off documentary we'd initially discussed.

Unknown to me, Tim had already got quite far down the line in negotiations with Sky Living. I thought it was still at the idea stage, but apparently they'd already started production of the *Steps Reunion* show without us knowing – Tim hadn't been clear about that.

So when I spoke to him about my concerns he said, 'Right, OK, I need to rethink this.'

'I'm not saying I don't want to do it, Tim,' I told him. 'I think a reunion would be great; I'm just saying I don't think that this is right.'

Tim was, in fact, moving to LA the next day to work on American *X Factor* – a small fact he'd neglected to tell us – which came as a shock. I just thought, 'How on earth are you going to manage doing that and look after us?'

The next I knew of it was when Tim sent me a text saying, 'Can you speak to the executive producer of the series? You owe him an explanation because they've already started paying people.'

I couldn't believe it!

'Well, that's not my fault,' I texted back, feeling my blood boil.

Things really kicked off after that and Tim told the others I didn't want to do a reunion show. It seemed like we'd already hit a fence before we'd even got going.

While all of this was happening I was still doing *Popstar To Operastar* as well, so I was training every day for that and getting bombarded with texts and emails because, understandably, everyone wanted to know what was going on. I'm sure they all thought, 'Claire was the one to push this and now she doesn't want to do it', so I was frantically emailing and texting the rest of the band saying, 'I'm not doing this to be awkward or nasty, but I've already said I'm not sure I have the time at the moment to commit so much time to a four- or five-part series. I didn't realize it had gone so far down the road, but I really do want to do something!'

Once I would have said, 'I'll get back into that band over my dead body!' but ten years had gone by; we were all older and wiser and we were all on friendly terms again. I was committed to it and I knew it was now or never. But I also felt like I'd been dropped in it and made to look like the bad guy again – while Tim had conveniently escaped to LA.

All of us in the band are pretty opinionated people, but the one thing we did all agree on from the start was that we wanted to do a tour. Tim had been very cautious about that and was really holding back on it, but we wanted it to happen. I honestly think Tim wanted to be involved simply because Steps was his baby – he'd been there from day one and didn't really want to give it up to anyone else. I think his attitude was that it was worth a go and if it was successful, then great. But we needed more than that – we needed to find another manager to coordinate everything and push projects along.

I was furious with him and annoyed with myself for trusting him when a few things hadn't gone right between us in the past. After I'd married Mark there was all the upset over our wedding photos. Then when I came back from my honeymoon I was meant to meet with him about doing a solo album – we'd even picked a few songs. I had thought he was working to set up a deal but I discovered nothing had been sorted. A couple of weeks after that, Tim's business partner Vicky rang me to say she was going back to New Zealand where she's from and they were splitting up the business. She didn't know what Tim was doing and he didn't call me to fill me in – well, not for a long time anyway.

Tim probably hates my guts now. I don't hate him but I did feel let down again. I said to the others, 'Look, we may need separate management as I can't work with Tim any more.' But the others all felt that they wanted to make the change as well – although the final decision was taken out of our hands as Tim decided to walk away.

I felt bad, though, because I'd persuaded H to agree to Tim being our manager and they hadn't spoken since their relationship broke up. I had to apologize to him and admit that it wasn't the right thing to have done. You live and learn.

We didn't particularly want anyone to know that we were thinking about a reunion and a tour, so we couldn't really go around town having meetings with managers. But we didn't know how to deal with all the things we were being offered – we were five separate entities. Luckily, a guy called Steven Howard was really keen to be involved. He was a founding director of Zomba, the umbrella company for Steps' record label, Jive. I didn't have much to do with Steven back in the early days of Steps, but he's done a great job with us and it's not easy, I can tell you! It's hard to be the person at the helm when you have five people with strong opinions who all think theirs is the most valid. But he believed in us and thought we had every chance of making a big impact.

I met the executive producer who'd been working on the *Steps Reunion* show for Sky Living and he pitched the idea for the series to me in person, and it all made a bit more sense – Tim had never really done that great a job of explaining things and making us feel confident that it was the right thing to do. He also told me that if it didn't happen now, then it probably never would. But he reassured me that they had no intention of damaging anyone's reputation or the memory of Steps, and that all they wanted to do was celebrate it. So, feeling a lot better about it all, *Steps Reunion* on Sky Living went into production.

Now all of us would have to sit round a table together for the first time in ten years and confront the past. We had to talk about the split if we had any hope of moving on, but I knew it wasn't going to be easy.

Although we'd been on speaking terms for a while and were friends again, dragging everything out into the open was bound to be painful. I still get very emotional and I think that gets mistaken for weakness, but I cry out of frustration because I find it hard to articulate how I feel when I'm put on the spot and have to defend myself. But I had to just keep reminding myself of how far I'd come: I was in a good place after doing *Popstar To Operastar*, I'd got to know myself a lot better since leaving Steps, and I'd made a proper life for myself with Reece and the kids. It was a world away from the person I'd been during those last days of Steps. And I really wanted this reunion to leave us with happy memories of the band, rather than it remaining something that would haunt us all forever. I wanted to rewrite the ending – for us, and our fans.

For the first episode of *Steps Reunion* we were taken to a beautiful hotel in the Cotswolds to have dinner. I hadn't really thought about how I would actually feel once I was in that situation and it was quite tough when Lisa, Lee and Faye started firing questions at me; and H and I did get upset. It all became very serious and, inevitably, the major issue was why we'd left Steps the way we did.

Lisa said, 'It was a shock. I was physically stunned,' and Faye said she was disappointed that her friends had let her down.

'That decision changed the course of five people's destinies,' Faye added. 'You didn't think about the three of us. Why couldn't you have come and discussed it?'

'Because we were barely talking to each other at the time,' I replied. 'H and I were travelling separately half the time.'

It's funny how people have such different perceptions of a situation, because I didn't feel we were friends at all at the time – we certainly weren't close and I didn't feel I could discuss anything with them. And if we'd been such good friends, then why had none of them noticed how miserable H and I were and how much we didn't want to be there? I think I did manage to get these points across to the other three, but maybe not quite as much as I should have done. All these years on, I was still shocked that none of them had picked up on our unhappiness. It's easy to gloss over things.

As for changing their destinies, how could I be responsible for their careers? I was twenty-four years old. Maybe Steps was still everything they'd ever dreamed of, but my dream had turned into a nightmare. My career didn't exactly soar after Steps was over, either – I didn't work after the H & Claire album and only got back into singing with *Popstar To Operastar*. In fact, my experience in Steps put me off singing for a long time: I completely lost my confidence because of the way I was made to feel about being chosen to sing lead vocals, but the others didn't get that.

'It felt like there was favouritism a lot of the time,' Lisa continued.

Faye nodded. 'I remember when you got asked to sing the whole of "One For Sorrow", I had this massive sinking feeling in my stomach, thinking, "Right, that means we're just backing singers",' she said.

Faye's comment hit a raw nerve in me. 'Everyone's reaction made me feel like absolute shit,' I hit back, unable to stop the tears from welling up.

I was just twenty when I recorded that song and I simply did what I was told. If any of the others had been in my situation they would have jumped at the opportunity to sing it – all of us were ambitious, all of us wanted to be successful. But I was made to feel that it was my fault I'd been given that song and that it wasn't my talent that put me in that situation, but the fact that I got on well with our management and producers.

The morning after the dinner, Faye knocked on my door. She was visibly upset. 'I felt like I was too hard on you last night,' she said, taking hold of my hand. 'I feel really bad about how it went.'

In the past I would have broken down, too, and would probably have been thinking to myself, 'Yeah, you were pretty horrible to me,' but I found that I actually didn't feel upset about it.

'Look, it doesn't matter,' I said. 'It won't make or break the reunion. I know it's a very emotional topic, so don't worry about it.'

It was a big step forward for me and, for the first time ever, I felt like I was a much stronger person than the Claire of old.

It still wasn't easy, though. As part of the show, Faye, Lisa and I went to Marbella for a girls' 'bonding' weekend. While we were sitting having a drink one day, I said I thought I'd been brave to tell them in person that I was leaving the band because I hate confrontation. Lisa shot back, 'I don't think it was brave, I think it was crazy.'

I didn't reply – I just hid behind my huge sunglasses and sipped my cocktail! They still didn't understand that, at the time, I felt getting out was my only option. If the situation had been different, maybe I would have done things differently, and I can see now that the way it was done wasn't necessarily the right way to do it, but I did what I thought was best for me at the time. I was young and I just wanted to leave. If I hadn't left when I did I would have completely destroyed myself and I dread to think where I'd be now. I honestly believe that's the way things were heading.

Looking back on my time with Steps, everything that happened – the good bits and the bad – all helped to make me who I am today and I'm a stronger person because of it. I'm not scared to ask questions and stick up for myself any more, and I think I can deal with things a lot better because I'm older. The things that would have upset me or bugged me ten years ago I wouldn't think of in the same way now because my priorities have changed. Ultimately, it's the kids and Reece who are most important to me and if anything I did with Steps were to threaten that, I would stop that immediately. Steps isn't my life any more, it's just what I do: it's my job, that's all. Reece and the kids are my life and that's the way it's got to be. If one of the kids was ill I'd have to say, 'I'm sorry, guys, but I have to go.'

I remember saying to Faye that while I love singing, I don't have that overwhelming urge to be in the spotlight or to court fame and publicity. Perhaps if I'd had that tunnel-vision kind of ambition, then my career and my life might have taken a very different path. But I just don't have the kind of pushiness that most other people in the business have.

I never expected the kind of fame I experienced in Steps. I hadn't trained for years to be a singer and there was always a part of me that felt I didn't deserve it or that other people felt I didn't deserve it: I'm sure that affected my self-confidence. I didn't have that tough outer shell that you need to deflect the negative comments and criticism that inevitably come with being in the public eye.

The fame side of things also put a lot of pressure on relationships within the band. One of the things that Lee and H said in the *Steps Reunion* series was that they wouldn't naturally have been friends had they not been thrown together in a band, and I think that was true of all of us. And when the pressure is on, those differences in personalities come to the fore. Part of the reason I'd felt so isolated was because Faye and Lisa both enjoyed socializing much more than I did. Wherever in the world we were on tour, they'd want to go out and experience the nightlife, while I just wanted to chill out at the hotel.

While we were making the *Reunion* series, we were offered a UK arena tour: twenty dates kicking off in Belfast in April 2012 that included the O2 in London. It was what we'd all wanted more than anything and we were so excited about it, but pretty nervous, too. It had been ten years since we'd last done it! Would people come to see us? Could we do it? Would I remember the dance moves? The Steps juggernaut was on the road again and gathering speed!

I was still a size 14–16, but I hadn't really thought about

my weight until the day we filmed our first dance rehearsal. They wanted us to get back in the studio to see if we could remember the routine to 'Tragedy', and we had to do it in front of the TV cameras. Gulp!

I hadn't been in a rehearsal studio for years and what immediately pinged into my head was, 'I've got nothing to wear!' First of all I decided, 'I'll just wear my exercise gear,' then I thought, 'You can't wear workout gear, Claire, you're going to look like an idiot! When pop stars go to rehearsals they look trendy!' Back in the day I'd worn combats with a little vest and trainers, but I hadn't bought anything like that in years.

I tried on loads of things and couldn't find anything to fit, so in the end I dragged out a pair of Miss Sixty camouflage combat trousers that I'd worn ten years ago, which used to sit really low on my hips. I got them on, but the waistband was now fitting snugly around my waist. I put a long grey T-shirt over them and hoped for the best. I even put a hairpiece in my hair, so I had a big ballerina bun.

When I got to the studio, though, and was standing in front of a mirrored wall, I just thought, 'Jesus, I look enormous!' and I really freaked out. I didn't want to join in with the dancing – I felt like a stroppy teenager. I know it's my issue and when I'm on my own I'm absolutely fine with my shape and know that I can wear certain things that suit me and I look good. But being back in that room with Faye and Lisa just took me back to all those body insecurities I'd felt years ago. H and Lee looked great too, which didn't help!

As far as I'm aware, no one else was thinking anything at all about how I looked, but my brain went into paranoid mode and I began obsessing: 'Oh God, they all think I'm really fat and everyone's looking at me because I'm bigger than them, and my grey T-shirt makes me look really frumpy, and EVERYTHING'S WOBBLING!' I just lost the plot a little bit, and really began to worry that I wasn't going to be able to do it. I didn't look like I had done ten years ago and I felt like an elephant – and an awkward one at that. Dancing isn't what I'm best at and while Faye, Lisa and H remembered all the moves, I felt like I was starting from scratch.

I'd made leaps and bounds in terms of improving my self-esteem after doing *Slave To Food* and appearing in *Popstar To Operastar*, and I didn't want to be back in that place where I felt shit about myself again. I never worried that I'd do what I did ten years before and starve myself, but I was a bit scared that I would go the other way again and start overeating to make myself feel better. I didn't want to be Fat Claire again. I also knew there was no way I would be fit enough to do the tour if I put on any more weight – I'd never get through a two-hour show.

Ten years ago I'd had age on my side and, although I was still only thirty-four, I hadn't actually performed like that since the day I left Steps. Faye and H had been doing musical theatre, Lisa had continued to do gigs as Lisa

Scott-Lee and Lee was a bloody fitness instructor! I, on the other hand, felt like a housewife who'd stumbled into a band by accident!

I was out of my comfort zone and it was a shock to the system. Until recently a typical day for me had revolved solely around the kids – getting them up, dressed, and fed, making Charlie's packed lunch and taking him to school. Daisy and I would go grocery shopping and pop into my sister's for a cuppa and a natter with her and my mum. All normal 'mum stuff'. The only dancing I did was playing *Just Dance* on the Wii with Gemma!

I found that it helped if I just kept telling myself that as the rehearsals went on, I'd get fitter and more confident, and that as soon as I got on the stage, the dance moves would all come flooding back and I'd love it. Plus Reece was really encouraging – he kept telling me I could do it and how proud he was of me. I know that secretly he couldn't wait for the first night of the tour.

As we got further into preparations for the album launch and the tour, I began to get more and more excited about the reunion. For the new compilation album, *The Ultimate Collection*, Steven thought it would be a good idea to do a bonus track, so we decided to cover the Abba classic 'Dancing Queen' – Pete Waterman had called us 'Abba on speed' after all, so we would be going back to our roots with the track!

Of course, it meant getting back in the recording studio for the first time in ten years, and I think everyone was a little tense about what would happen when it came to sharing out the vocals. Our producer Eliot Kennedy was great, though. He knew the history of the band and the problems that had been caused when I'd been given most of the lines to sing. He understood it was an emotional subject for all of us and he really helped us to feel more relaxed about the session.

There was one moment in the studio where we were discussing the vocals and Lisa said, 'I don't think Claire should start the song. I think it would build nicely with Faye or me and then Claire.'

Quite a lot was made of that on the *Reunion* show, but I actually agreed with Lisa – she was right and it did work better with Faye starting the track.

Before Faye turned up for the session, Eliot asked Lisa and me to sing together in the booth, which was quite a big moment for us. Ten years ago, I could never have imagined that happening, but it actually felt really good to be back in the studio, having a laugh with everyone. I never thought I'd ever feel that way again and it was really nice.

Once the track had been recorded, the next thing on our to-do list was getting new publicity shots done, so we were sent to the studio with image consultant Vernon François, who styles the likes of Jessie J.

Once we'd all found the right outfits and been made up for the shoot I felt so choked up. We asked the photographer to turn the monitor round so we could see how we looked in the photo and I just lost it and started crying. I never, ever thought I'd see us all looking like that again.

I know it was my fault that there had been every chance it would never happen again, but even though I'd walked out of the band it still meant so much to me. It had been a huge part of my life. It had *changed* my life. To see us all looking like a band again was almost like cancelling out the past ten years. It didn't feel weird at all – we'd all just slipped back into it like we'd done it yesterday.

Around the release of *The Ultimate Collection* we planned a few TV appearances and interviews, and the first was a live performance of 'Tragedy' and 'It's The Way You Make Me Feel' on ITV1's *This Morning*.

I was absolutely terrified and my legs were shaking as we walked into the TV studio to take our positions. At the beginning of the song we had to do a turn and I had these great big high-heeled shoes on and was convinced I wouldn't make it through the performance without falling on my bum and making a complete idiot of myself. But it was a good performance and I was really surprised by how much I enjoyed singing 'Tragedy'. Ten years ago I think we'd all got to the point where we thought, 'Oh God, do we have to do this again?' but when we performed it on *This Morning*, I loved every minute of it. There were so many people behind the cameras watching us with huge grins on their faces, including the show's presenters Holly Willoughby and Phillip Schofield. That kind of joyful energy was what Steps had been all about for the fans, and it felt brilliant.

*

Our new compilation album *The Ultimate Collection* was released on 10 October 2011, almost ten years to the day after the release of our *Gold: Greatest Hits* album. It, too, went straight to number one.

We were all together having a celebration dinner for the record launch with our manager Steven when we heard the news that the album had hit the top spot. I don't remember us ever being together when the chart was announced in the past, so it was fantastic to be in the same room this time and we all got very emotional. It meant so much more because it had been ten years since our last number-one album. It felt unreal, and none of us could quite believe we were back at the top of the charts again.

The *Steps Reunion* series had been a hit, too, and I'm not too proud to admit I'd been wrong about that. And, to top it all off, Steven told us that our tour had sold 100,000 tickets in the first forty-eight hours. I think all of us felt a bit overwhelmed that our fans were still out there and wanted to come and see us after so many years of being away. We'd be nowhere without them.

This dinner felt so different to the first one we'd had at the start of the reunion. The tension had gone, we were laughing and joking with each other and talking excitedly about the future, instead of wallowing in the past. We were friends.

'To Steps!' shouted H, as we all clinked our champagne glasses together. We were back!

FINAL WORD

REWRITING THE ENDING

Writing this book has been an eye-opening experience for me. Looking back on my life has made me realize quite how far I've come from the fresh-faced teen full of hopes and dreams for the future, who walked into that hall in Surrey in 1997 to audition for Steps.

Some of the memories have made me laugh, some have made me cry and some have been really hard to revisit, but all of them have made me see that I've got a hell of a lot to be grateful for and I can say with my hand on my heart that I'm the most content I've ever been. It's helped to put everything into perspective.

I have the family I've always dreamed of – two beautiful kids and an amazing husband who's a wonderful father and who's never failed to support me through fat times, thin times and when my career has hit rock bottom. My family means the world to me – they've given me everything I've ever wanted. They've made me the important person I always hoped I would be. I don't have to try to impress them – all I have to do is be myself for Charlie and Daisy to think I'm the greatest thing since sliced bread, and it's a really lovely feeling. And, who knows, maybe we'll add another little one to our brood – I've always imagined myself with a gang of kids around me!

Things have settled down between my mum and dad, Nina and Bob. Dad lives in Cyprus some of the time and, although I hate him being away, he loves it out there. My sister Gemma and her partner Peter have three lovely kids, Poppy, Peter and Mitchel. And I'm learning to be a better step-parent, too. Olivia is a teenager now and when she comes to stay she'd rather talk to me about girls' stuff than Reece. All I can hope for is that we'll be friends, because I know that's all I should be. Maybe I can be the person she'll come to when she doesn't want to talk to her parents! And it helps that I'm a pop star – that's given me lots of Brownie points. I remember when she was little she drew a picture of us singing and wrote that because I was famous I was going to make her a pop star too, one day. I think she quite likes to say to her American friends, 'My stepmum's famous in England.' It gives her something to brag about.

One of the most important things my family has given me is an identity away from the band. I think there are two Claires – there's 'Claire from Steps' and there's Claire Richards; and it's the Claire Richards part that keeps me sane and grounded, and makes me able to cope with being a pop star. I didn't have that ten years ago – Steps was my entire life and when that started to go wrong, I lost my way as I had nothing to fall back on. I can see now that Steps is just my job and I'm very lucky to be doing something I enjoy. Not many people have that.

I wanted to go on our 2012 tour and have the time of my life and bring my family along, too. I wanted to be able to look back on it with good memories rather than bad ones. And this time around I saw a real change in myself – I wasn't afraid to speak up any more and I was really proud of myself for that. I hope I'll now have the confidence to do other projects away from Steps – as I loved my time on *Popstar To Operastar* so much, maybe I'll get the chance to do my own album. I'd love that.

What's also great is that I'm known for more than being in Steps these days. When people recognize me in the street now, it's usually from *Slave To Food*, and their comments are only ever positive. I've had so many women come up to me and say how great I look and how much they loved the show. One lady said to me, 'It's so nice for normal mums to see celebrities like you struggle with the same things we do.' It was wonderful and I started crying immediately, of course! I've never had that before and it's so much nicer than someone saying, 'Weren't you the girl in that band?'

I hope I've put my weight issues behind me. Nowadays, my weight isn't the first thing I think about every morning – I don't wake up worrying if I'm going to fit into my clothes. If I want to have a glass of wine, I'll have one. I'm not perfect, but I think I've finally got my body image into perspective. It's not the end of the world if I'm a size 16 – I'd prefer to be a size 12, but if that doesn't happen then that's OK. And because I've been every single size in the spectrum over the past fifteen years – from a size 8 to a 20 – I know I'm not happy being a size 8 and I know I'm not happy at a size 20. But I do know I can be happy being a size 12, 14 or even a 16! My life doesn't have to stop because of my size any more. I'm learning to love my curves and I don't mind wearing a tighter dress if it shows my shape.

I'm sure I'll still have moments of insecurity – going back into Steps made me doubt myself a little. But when I walked out onto that stage for the first of our arena shows, I was wearing a size 14 outfit and I was OK with it because I'm happy being Claire Richards now.

The career I wished for as a kid is back again, and I'm incredibly lucky to get a second chance. I have so many other things in my life now and I know it doesn't all rest on my career with Steps. As long as I can juggle it all and keep everyone happy, then this next year will hopefully be the most amazing I've ever had.

I'm confident the next chapter of my life is going to be bigger and better and, if the going gets tough, I always know I'll feel a hell of a lot better if I'm wearing two pairs of Spanx!

Acknowledgements

I'd like to thank the following people:

Reece, thank you for always being there and supporting me, you truly are my best friend and my soulmate. I couldn't do any of this without you and I honestly wouldn't want to. I love you so much. x

My beautiful babies Charlie and Daisy, for making being your mummy the most wonderful, fulfilling experience of my life. The love and joy you bring me every single day makes everything else pale in comparison. I love you with every little bit of my heart. x

My mum and dad, for always supporting me and my decisions, and teaching me how to be a good parent. Without you I wouldn't be the person I am today. I love you both so so much. x

My little sister Gemma, who is not only my sister but my best friend. You are a very special person, Mrs, and so loved by everyone. Believe in yourself as much as you believe in me and you'll be unstoppable. I love you. x

To my whole family, old and new. From Karaoke to the O2 you've always been there to cheer me on and support me, so thank you. Auntie Pauline you are missed terribly every day; I wish you were here to see this chapter in all our lives. x

Faye, Lee, Lisa and H, we have been on the most amazing journey together and I'm so glad it isn't over yet. x

Neil Howarth of Urban Associates, you believed in me when I couldn't believe in myself. Thank you for all the opportunities you've brought me. x

All my friends, you know who you are! Thank you for never expecting me to be anything other than who I've always been. You mean so much to me. x

Claire Higney – who helped me put my story into words and bring it to life. Thank you. x

Everyone at my publishers, Pan Macmillan. x